William Faulkner's

The Sound and the Fury

Text by
Boria Sax
(Ph.D., SUNY Buffalo)
Department of English
Mercy College
Dobbs Ferry, NY

Illustrations by
Thomas E. Cantillon

 Research & Education Association

What MAXnotes® Will Do for You

This book is intended to help you absorb the essential contents and features of William Faulkner's *The Sound and The Fury* and to help you gain a thorough understanding of the work. The book has been designed to do this more quickly and effectively than any other study guide.

For best results, this **MAXnotes** book should be used as a companion to the actual work, not instead of it. The interaction between the two will greatly benefit you.

To help you in your studies, this book presents the most up-to-date interpretations of every section of the actual work, followed by questions and fully explained answers that will enable you to analyze the material critically. The questions also will help you to test your understanding of the work and will prepare you for discussions and exams.

Meaningful illustrations are included to further enhance your understanding and enjoyment of the literary work. The illustrations are designed to place you into the mood and spirit of the work's settings.

The **MAXnotes** also include summaries, character lists, explanations of plot, and section-by-section analyses. A biography of the author and discussion of the work's historical context will help you put this literary piece into the proper perspective of what is taking place.

The use of this study guide will save you the hours of preparation time that would ordinarily be required to arrive at a complete grasp of this work of literature. You will be well prepared for classroom discussions, homework, and exams. The guidelines that are included for writing papers and reports on various topics will prepare you for any added work which may be assigned.

The **MAXnotes** will take your grades "to the max."

Dr. Max Fogiel
Program Director

Contents

> **Each Part includes List of Characters,
> Summary, Analysis, Study Questions and
> Answers, and Suggested Essay Topics.**

Introduction

The Life and Work of William Faulkner

Troubled young people may find some inspiration in the life of William Faulkner. He overcame more than a full share of hesitations, mistakes, false starts, poor luck and even defects of character to become the most celebrated American novelist of the twentieth century. Born in 1897 in the rural town of New Albany, Mississippi, Faulkner was taken as a child to the nearby university town of Oxford, where his father received a modest administrative post. He was a poor student, who failed to finish high school. When World War I broke out, he tried to enlist in the army but was rejected as too thin and weak. Not one to give up easily, he crossed the border and enlisted in the Royal Canadian Air Force. He proved, however, to be an inept pilot who crashed twice and never was sent into battle.

Despite his poor record in school, Faulkner decided early that he wished to be a writer, but for a long time he knew neither what sort of thing he wished to write nor how to support himself. After the war, he returned to Oxford and enrolled for a while at the local university. He received mediocre grades in most subjects but flunked English. His early manhood was spent in a series of jobs, from delivering mail to shoveling coal. None worked out well and, after a while, he would either quit or else get fired.

Like many other aspiring authors of the early 1920s, Faulkner went to live in Greenwich Village, the Bohemian section of New York City. The stay was brief and generally lonely, except that he met the writer Sherwood Anderson, who offered valuable guidance.

Anderson encouraged Faulkner to focus his literary efforts on the region where he was raised, most especially the Southern storytelling traditions.

After returning once again to Oxford, Faulkner eventually managed to publish a book of poems and a few novels, which sold modestly well but received no critical attention. Then an intense burst of inspiration produced his first major work, *The Sound and the Fury* in 1929 (also the year of his marriage). This novel not only began to bring Faulkner to the attention of the literary public, but it also inaugurated a period of extraordinary creativity which was to last about a decade and a half.

Several more works followed in rapid succession including such critically acclaimed novels as *Light in August* (1932) and *Absalom, Absalom* (1936). He also wrote several collections of short stories including *Go Down, Moses*, which contained "The Bear," a novella of a young man preparing for life on the frontier which vanishes as he comes to maturity.

Recognition, however, came to Faulkner very slowly. While some critics felt his work contained high drama and themes of nearly Biblical dimensions, others accused Faulkner of being merely sensational. It was not until the late forties that his reputation as a leading American novelist became established. In 1950, Faulkner received the Nobel Prize for literature.

In his final decade Faulkner settled comfortably into a role as an elder statesman of American letters. His fiction became somewhat less pessimistic, though most critics feel that the energy of his early writing was gone. Since his death in 1962, however, his reputation has survived many changes in critical fashions.

Historical Background

Perhaps no other modern author in any country has succeeded quite so well as Faulkner in combining an intimate knowledge of traditional rural life with the themes and experiments of the literary avant-garde. Though he remained a regional author, only occasionally venturing outside of Mississippi, his novels are the most celebrated example of "high modernism" in American fiction.

The early decades of the twentieth century, as Faulkner came to maturity, were a period of extraordinary innovation and excitement in the arts. Inspired in part by the work of physicists like Einstein, artists and writers attempted to challenge received notions of time and space. In Europe, cubist painters tried to represent objects from several angles simultaneously, while futurists tried to show several moments in time at once. Surrealists challenged the boundary between fantasy and reality, and Dadaists placed in question the very legitimacy of art itself.

The modernists, a loose alliance of cultural movements, sought to replace traditional artistic forms with new ways of organizing experience. The way human beings experience the world, they pointed out, is far more fluid than a simple chronology. It is a blend of sensation, memory, anticipation, emotion and thought, which can sometimes become almost indistinguishable. In attempts to render the flow of experience, poets like T. S. Eliot broke down traditional forms. Others such as e. e. cummings even rejected traditional syntax.

In prose, the most discussed attempt to bring narrative closer to experience was a technique known as "stream of consciousness." This consisted of presenting the subjective reality of individuals through loosely connected associations rather than recording factual events. Several writers developed this technique almost simultaneously, but most critics feel it culminated in the novel *Ulysses* by James Joyce, first published in 1922, which sensuously described the perceptions of a man during a fairly ordinary day in Dublin, Ireland.

The most influential modernists were sophisticated cosmopolitans who lived in the great cultural centers of Europe such as London, Berlin, Vienna, Moscow and, above all, Paris. They felt an exhilaration at the rapid pace of intellectual and social change, even if they also feared the future. Faulkner, like virtually every aspiring young writer, made a pilgrimage to Paris as a young man. Though he returned somewhat disenchanted, Faulkner brought the techniques and concerns of the modernist to the literature of a region that was considered "backward" and "provincial." After reading *Ulysses*, he began to write *The Sound and the Fury*.

The South that Faulkner wrote about impressed more superficial observers as, depending on their point of view, a rural paradise or a bastion of prejudice and narrow-mindedness. Faulkner, with his intimate knowledge of the region, uncovered tensions as complex and dramatic as those of any great Metropolis.

The memory of slavery, Faulkner found, lingered in the South as an ancestral curse, a sort of regional original sin. As a consequence of this, harmonious human relationships were extremely difficult, often impossible. The legacy of this institution remained as racial segregation and as an atmosphere of violence. While slavery was seldom mentioned, associations with it constantly surfaced. Nearly everything in society, in consequence, appeared sullied and degraded.

Sexual relationships, most especially, were complicated by this brutal legacy. The white masters had often amused themselves sexually with female black slaves, something that the mixed complexions of many people constantly brought to mind. For many people, both black and white, this suggested racial pollution. Genetic or social defects of individuals might be blamed on obscure rumors of such liaisons.

The people in Faulkner's fiction respond to this sense of corruption in various ways. Some seek solace in religion, while others are consumed with rage. Some become embittered and cynical, and still more try to counter the corruption with romantic ideals.

At times, the search for purity culminates in a cult of Southern womanhood. The high value placed on virginity of elite young ladies reflects a longing for lost innocence. The chivalrous ideal appealed to a culture that was still largely agrarian, aristocratic and almost feudal. It placed, however, an unrealistic burden on women, which could lead to bitter conflicts.

Faulkner also realized that the South was changing in ways that were, perhaps, more subtle yet no less comprehensive than the changes coming to more heavily industrialized areas. As the generations raised under slavery died out, racial segregation was no longer universally accepted. Furthermore, the aristocrats were gradually being forced to cede power to the bourgeoisie, and traditional values were corrupted by the pursuit of money.

Though far too knowledgeable and sophisticated to romanticize the old South unduly, Faulkner often seemed to sympathize with the claims of tradition. Though he endorsed the civil rights movement of the 1950s, Faulkner never showed more than a very casual interest in political matters. He was far more interested in dramatizing problems than in searching for solutions. In his most highly regarded works at least, his view is fundamentally tragic.

The most celebrated writers often disregard all the rules that students of literature are expected to observe, and Faulkner is one of the best examples. His critics have had little difficulty in finding things to complain about. Faulkner would sometimes write convoluted sentences, filled with relative clauses in which the pronouns could not be linked with any identifiable antecedents. He seemed, furthermore, to dwell morbidly on obsessions with such subjects as incest, castration and senseless violence. His language is sometimes archaic and, many feel, overly florid.

Such criticisms caused the work of Faulkner to be neglected for much of his life, and similar complaints are still not uncommon today. Faulkner, however, had a wonderful ear for dialogue and an eye for sensual detail. He had fine control over the rhythms of his prose, which can be terse and dramatic or expansive and sensual. He was able to handle great themes of guilt and redemption. Finally, his defenders feel that his works are animated by a passion which renders their technical shortcomings nearly insignificant.

Master List of Characters

I. Members of the Compson Family:

Jason Compson III—*the scion of an aristocratic family, husband of Caroline and father of Jason IV, Benjy, Quentin and Caddy. He constantly tells his children that all human endeavor is futile, and that it does not truly matter what a person does. He dies in 1912.*

Caroline Compson—*the wife of Jason Compson III and mother of the Compson children. She is constantly talking of her own death, which she believes is imminent. Deprived of other psychological supports, she values stability above all else. She banishes Caddy from her home for promiscuity, and she prefers Jason, whom she believes to be most normal, over her other children.*

Caddy (Candace) Compson—*the second of the Compson children and mother of Miss Quentin. She offers emotional support to* her brothers Benjy and Quentin, who both become obsessed with her. She has several affairs, including one with Dalton Ames, who may be the father of Miss Quentin. She then marries Herbert Head, who, on learning of her pregnancy, abandons her. She is then also banished from the Compson house.

Benjy (at first "Maury," name changed to "Benjamin") Compson— *the profoundly retarded son of Jason III and Caroline, and their youngest child. Though he cannot speak, the first section of the novel is told from his point of view. He often seems to have an instinctive wisdom, and his cries express the tragedy of the Compson household.*

Quentin Compson (Dan)—*the eldest child of the Compson family, son of Jason III and Caroline, brother of Caddy, Benjy and Jason III. The second section of the novel is told from his point of view. Despite going to Harvard, he remains obsessed with his sister and her loss of virginity, which, for him, symbolizes all the corruption of the world. He commits suicide by jumping in the Charles River.*

Jason Compson IV—*the third child of the Compson family, son of Jason III and Caroline, brother of Caddy, Quentin (male) and Benjamin. The third section of the novel is told from his point of view. He is so filled with rage that there seems to be no room for any other passion, and he lashes out against virtually everyone he encounters. He embezzles money sent by Caddy for her daughter Quentin, who, in turn, steals his savings and runs away.*

Damuddy—*the mother of Caroline Compson, dead since 1898.*

Maury Bascomb (Uncle Maury)—*the brother of Caroline. Alcoholic and irresponsible, he is constantly taking money from his sister. Initially, Benjy was named "Maury" after him, but the name was changed after the child's retardation was discovered.*

Miss Quentin—*the daughter of Caddy, possibly conceived with Dalton Ames. She is constantly tormented by Jason IV, who also steals money that Caddy sends for her. Quentin finally retaliates by stealing the savings of Jason and running away with a travelling performer.*

II. Negro Servants in the Compson House:

Dilsey Gibson—*the most clearly positive character in the book, Dilsey is the wife of Roskus Gibson, mother of T.P., Versh and Frony and the grandmother of Luster. In the Compson house, she defends Benjy and Miss Quentin against mistreatment by Jason IV, even though her compassion is generally not reciprocated. In the final section of the book, she is generally the main character. Her ability to endure and retain her humanity despite the brutality that surrounds her does much to soften the pessimistic tone of the book.*

Frony Gibson—*daughter of Dilsey and Roskus and mother of Luster. She seems to take little interest in her son, but she is very concerned about propriety.*

Luster Gibson—*son of Frony and grandson of Dilsey and Roskus, he holds major responsibility for taking care of Benjy. Despite mistreatment by Jason IV and others, he manages to retain his good humor.*

Roskus Gibson—*husband of Dilsey, and father of T.P., Versh and Frony. After being nearly incapacitated with rheumatism, dies around 1914.*

T.P. Gibson—*the eldest son of Roskus and Dilsey. He is a good-natured man, who helps out with a variety of tasks.*

Versh Gibson—*the second son of Dilsey and Roskus. He looks after Benjy until Luster takes over. Versh is superstitious and tells Benjy that the name makes him into a "bluegum" or sorcerer.*

III. Other Characters:

Dalton Ames—*a seducer of Caddy and possible father of Miss Quentin, who views women with contempt. Quentin (male), attempting to defend his sister's honor, picks a fight with Dalton Ames, but Ames defeats Caddy's brother effortlessly.*

Anse—*the sheriff in a town near Cambridge, Mass., who arrests Quentin for allegedly abducting a little girl.*

Gerald Bland—*a student at Harvard, who devotes himself to boxing and seducing young ladies. Quentin (male) picks a fight with him, but Gerald defeats his adversary without trouble.*

Mrs. Bland—*the mother of Gerald and a constant defender of male privilege. She defends Quentin (male) against the charge of abducting a child, but she takes pride in her son's sexual conquests.*

Three Boys—*encountered by Quentin (male) as he wanders about Cambridge, Mass. They dream of winning a reward by catching a huge trout, but, rather than trying, they decide to go swimming.*

Charlie—*an early boyfriend of Caddy who shares a swing with her.*

Deacon—*a Negro at Harvard from the South, to whom Quentin (male) entrusts his suicide note.*

Earl—*the employer of Jason IV. He is troubled by the lack of time spent by Jason at work and suspects him of questionable financial dealing, but he does not wish to fire Jason out of regard for Mrs. Compson.*

Little Italian Girl—*a young girl who gets lost and whom Quentin (male) attempts to help, only to be accused by her brother of abduction.*

Herbert Head—*becomes engaged to marry Caddy and promises Jason IV a position at his bank. On learning Caddy is not a virgin, he breaks the engagement and rescinds his promise to Jason IV.*

Uncle Job—*an African-American who works alongside of Jason IV. He constantly angers his colleague with a casual approach to work, but Earl considers him very reliable.*

Lorraine—*a prostitute whom Jason IV visits in Memphis on weekends. Though Jason speaks of her, like everyone else, with contempt she is able to manipulate him for money. He does not want their relationship known and forbids her to call him at work.*

Old Man—*he is with a troop of travelling entertainers. After Jason IV, searching for his niece and her money, calls the old man a "liar," the man runs after him with an axe.*

The Man with the Red Tie—*a member of the troop of travelling entertainers, recognized by his red tie. He eventually helps Miss Quentin run away.*

Natalie—*an early girlfriend of Quentin, who arouses the anger of Caddy.*

Jeweler—*a man whom Quentin visits to ask if the watch from his father can be repaired.*

Mrs. Patterson—*a married woman with whom Uncle Maury is having an affair.*

Mr. Patterson—*the husband of Mrs. Patterson. He learns of Uncle Maury's affair with his wife and assaults Uncle Maury.*

Shreve MacKenzie—*a roommate of Quentin (male) at Harvard who comes from Canada (also a character in Faulkner's* Absalom, Absalom).

Spoade—*a fellow student of Quentin (male) and Shreve MacKenzie at Harvard, who has a reputation for laziness.*

Squire—*a public official who tries Quentin after he has been charged with abducting a young girl in Cambridge. He takes a very casual approach to the law, makes no judgement but requires Quentin to pay six dollars.*

Rev. Shegog—*a pastor who preaches a sermon that moves parishioners at the Negro church in Jefferson to tears.*

Troop Manager—*looks after the travelling entertainers and rescues Jason IV after one of the troop has assaulted Jason with an axe.*

Summary of the Novel

The Sound and the Fury consists of four sections, linked by a common set of characters and themes. Each might be read as an autonomous work. They all tell episodes in the decline of the Compson family, but are only loosely connected. Furthermore, the first three sections are presented from the perspective of characters whose impressions may not necessarily be reliable. Any re-construction of the action is, therefore, somewhat uncertain.

The first section is dated April 7, 1928, the birthday of Benjy and the day before Easter. It is told from the perspective of Benjy, who is severely retarded, and consists mostly of sensual impressions blended with memories. These range throughout his entire life, from relatively happy times with his sister Caddy and brothers Quentin and Jason to his castration for a clumsy sexual approach to a girl.

The second section is dated June 2, 1910, and is narrated from the point of view of Benjy's brother Quentin. Like the previous section, it blends the present and the past, but it records a relatively continuous chain of events. Quentin is at Harvard, and has decided to commit suicide. Before he does it, however, he wanders through Cambridge, having adventures, reminiscing and getting into a fight. He thinks, above all, of his sister Caddy and his obsession with her loss of virginity. Finally, he drowns himself in the Charles River.

The third section is dated Friday, April 6, 1928 and narrated by Jason Compson IV, brother of Caddy, Benjy and Quentin. He cheats and embezzles from all the female members of his family—his mother, Mrs. Compson; his sister, Caddy; his niece, Miss Quentin. But, though obsessed with money, he is an inept businessman whose circumstances remain fairly marginal.

The final section is narrated in the third person and dated Easter Sunday, April 8, 1928. Miss Quentin steals the money that Jason IV has embezzled from her together with the rest of his savings to run away with a circus performer. Jason is more furious than ever. The section focuses, however, on the housekeeper Dilsey, who manages to maintain her dignity and perspective through all the trials and tribulations.

Estimated Reading Time

The Sound and the Fury is a difficult text even for scholars who are used to literary experiments. It is best, however, not to feel intimidated. The reader who has some idea of what to expect will be far more comfortable with the book.

It is necessary, above all, to lay aside our expectations of a logical sequence of events. The first two parts, most especially, blend past and present, sensation and memory, dream and reality. Though some scenes are relatively clear, we are not always quite certain what is happening. The reader must, therefore, be willing to accept something short of complete understanding. Some may feel disoriented and confused. Those who can relax with the novel will be far better able to enjoy the vividness of the dialogue and description.

The reader must, in other words, first accept the novel on its own terms and not expect a traditional narrative. If the sense of a passage seems unclear, it is best to simply read on so as not to interrupt the flow of images and ideas. Then, if he or she desires, the reader may return later to the difficult passage and reconstruct what it meant. The reader should not worry too much about the details. He or she ought to concentrate instead on understanding important themes.

Before beginning the novel, the reader should also consider, as honestly as possible, just what his or her reason for reading it is. There are many possible motivations. Are you reading it simply to fulfill a school assignment and get a decent grade? Are you reading it for enjoyment? Out of curiosity? Do you wish to learn about literature in general? Are you interested in American history or Southern culture? Are you searching for wisdom? Are you intrigued by interpersonal dynamics?

Most readers will have a combination of motives, but which are more important? The novel may be approached in many ways. If you are aware of your motivations, you will know what sort of details to look for. You will also have a better idea of how much effort to expend. Generally, those readers whose reasons are complex and numerous will take longer than others to finish the novel. They will also find the experience more rewarding.

The best way to read *The Sound and the Fury* is to devote a session to each section. This should help the reader grasp the internal unity of each part. Those who read less at a session risk missing the connections between scenes. Those who read more at a session risk being unnecessarily confused.

If the reader takes an average of one hour and forty five minutes per session, the four sections will require a total reading time of seven hours. This is, however, a very rough expectation. Much will depend, as already noted, on the purposes of the reading.

A single reading will be enough to give a good idea of the style and content of *The Sound and the Fury*, but it will certainly not enable the reader to understand everything. Many scenes can only be appreciated in retrospect, when one knows about consequences that are only apparent later in the novel. In addition to being aware of his or her purpose, the reader should also decide what level of understanding to be satisfied with. Many people feel moved to reread the book several times over a period of many years.

There are some minor disputes among scholars as to exactly what the correct text of certain passages in *The Sound and the Fury* should be. A surviving carbon copy of the manuscript as typed by Faulkner does not always correspond to the original edition, and it is uncertain which changes may have been authorized by the author.

In addition, Faulkner wrote a brief supplement to the novel for *The Portable Faulkner*, edited by Malcolm Crowley and first published in 1945. Most scholars, however, do not regard this as part of the novel. It contradicts the original text on some points, indicating that Faulkner probably did not remember his own narrative terribly well.

This study guide has been written following the text in the Vintage Books edition (1984), edited by Noel Polk, which is both highly regarded and easy to obtain. This discussion has been presented in such a way as to not make the reader dependent on the pagination in this or any other printed copy of the novel.

Part One

Benjy: April 7, 1928

New Characters:

Maury Bascomb: *brother of Mrs Caroline Compson. He is having an affair with Mrs Patterson*

Benjy Compson (Maury, Benjamin): *a profoundly retarded man, from whose perspective the section is narrated. He is the youngest son in the Compson family; brother of Caddy, Quentin (male) and Jason IV*

Caddy (Candace) Compson: *daughter of Mr and Mrs Compson, sister of Benjy, Quentin (male) and Caddy*

Mrs Caroline Compson: *mother of Benjy, Caddy, Quentin (male) and Jason IV*

Jason Compson III: *father of Benjy, Caddy, Quentin (male) and Jason IV*

Jason Compson IV: *son of Mr and Mrs Compson, brother of Benjy, Caddy and Quentin*

Quentin (Dan) Compson: *eldest son of Mr and Mrs Compson; brother of Benjy, Caddy, and Jason IV*

Damuddy: *the maternal grandmother of the Compson children, who dies in 1898*

Frony: *daughter of Dilsey and Roskus Gibson, sister of T.P. and Versh, mother of Luster*

Dilsey Gibson: *the aging cook and housekeeper in the Compson house, wife of Roskus, mother of T.P., Versh, and Frony*

Roskus Gibson: *the husband of Dilsey, father of T.P., Versh, and Frony, who dies in about 1914*

T. P. Gibson: *eldest son of Dilsey and Roskus, brother of Versh and Frony*

Versh Gibson: *second son of Dilsey and Roskus, brother of Frony and T.P., who takes care of Benjy before the task is delegated to Luster*

Luster: *a young Negro servant, whose job is to look after Benjy*

Mrs Patterson: *the wife of Mr Patterson. She is having an affair with Maury Bascomb*

Mr Patterson: *the husband of Mrs Patterson, who assaults Maury Bascomb for carrying on an affair with his wife*

Miss Quentin: *the daughter of Caddy, whom Luster and Benjy see climbing down a pear tree out of her room*

Summary

This section is narrated from the point of view of Benjy, a severely retarded man on his thirty-third birthday. It consists of memories mixed with impressions, and moves back and forth between different periods of time. It is the most difficult part of the book, and scholars do not always agree on exactly what is happening in the narrative. They have divided it into events in various ways, usually into about 12 to 15 stories. Some of these, however, are linked only by associated places and objects, while others can be combined in longer sequences of events. There are roughly 100 changes of scene. Originally, Faulkner asked that the section be coded through print in various colors to indicate the different events. This was, however, too difficult and expensive for his publisher. Today, it would not be nearly so hard to mark the sections with colors or at least different fonts. No major publisher has attempted this, in part because of controversy over how the sections might be divided up. The transition from one set of events to an-

other is generally indicated by italics, but these are not used in a
very consistent manner.

There are a few major events, however, that stand out, and the
reader should use them as points of orientation. These are the
following:

On the Golf Course (present time)

The novel begins on a golf course after Benjy, together with
Luster who looks after him, has climbed in through a hole in the
fence. As we will learn in part two of the novel, the property is an
area which was once known as "Benjy's pasture," because he was
sent there to play as a child and as a young man. It was later sold to
pay for his brother Quentin's college tuition to Harvard, but Benjy
retains a fondness for it.

It is the day before Easter, and it is also Benjy's thirty-third
birthday. A golfer calls out the word "caddie," which is also the name
of Benjy's sister who has been away for a long time. Thinking of
her makes Benjy begin to cry. Luster manages to calm Benjy by
reminding him of the birthday cake that the servant Dilsey is making, then threatening to eat the entire cake, candles and all, if Benjy
does not behave.

Luster is busy looking all over for a quarter he lost through a
hole in his pocket. He needs the money to go to a minstrel show
that night. When nobody else will help him, Luster asks Benjy to
look out for the quarter. He takes Benjy down to a stream to search,
then takes off Benjy's shoes for wading. Everything triggers memories for Benjy, and he, accordingly, becomes upset from time to
time. At one point he finds a golf ball and wishes to play with it,
but Luster refuses to let him and pockets the ball.

They come to a swing and Benjy sees Miss Quentin, the daughter of his sister Caddy, with a boyfriend. Benjy approaches and Miss
Quentin tells him to go away. The boyfriend, who wears a red tie, is
friendly and entertains Benjy with a trick. He puts a lighted match
in his mouth then takes it out, still burning. When he asks Benjy to
try it, Miss Quentin stops him then runs away. After talking briefly
with Luster, he learns how Miss Quentin climbs out of her room.

Benjy is calm for a while, but then he begins to cry again. Luster quiets Benjy by giving him a flower. Then, to tease him, Luster

takes the flower away and Benjy moans again. Luster takes Benjy home, and the housekeeper Dilsey brings him into the kitchen. Watching the fire, he grows calm.

Then Benjy celebrates his birthday together with the Negro servants. Dilsey has made a cake, and Luster blows the candles out for Benjy. Then Mrs Compson, Benjy's mother, comes down to complain about the noise.

Soon it is time for dinner. The Compsons are seated at a table. When Benjy, once again, starts to cry, Miss Quentin complains about Benjy, saying that he ought to be locked up. This is followed by bitter arguments between Miss Quentin and Jason IV, during which Benjy is soon forgotten.

After dinner, when getting ready for bed, Benjy looks in the mirror and cries again. Then he and Luster look out the window to see Miss Quentin running away with the man in the red tie. Benjy thinks of his sister Caddy and grows calm.

The Compson Children (1898)

When Benjy gets in the stream it first triggers a memory from a day when he was three years old and played with his sister and two brothers. At the time, he was called "Maury" after his uncle.

Caddy, who is seven, gets her dress wet in the stream. Versh, a black servant who is taking care of Benjy, tells Caddy that her mother will whip her because of the dress. Caddy decides to take her dress off and dry it. Her brother Quentin, who is nine, objects, but the opposition only makes Caddy more determined. She tells Versh to unbutton her dress, threatening to reveal secrets if he refuses.

With the help of Versh, Caddy takes off her dress and tosses it on the bank, so she is wearing only her bodice and drawers. Quentin slaps Caddy, who falls into the water. She splashes Quentin, who splashes back. Versh takes Benjy away, then threatens to tell on Caddy and Quentin. Caddy's drawers are covered with mud.

Roskus, the husband of Dilsey, calls the children to supper. Quentin worries about the punishment in store for them, but Caddy defiantly says that she hopes they will get whipped. After putting her dress back on, Quentin hopes that Versh and Jason will

not tell their parents what happened, but Caddy insists she does not care.

Caddy moves boldly on ahead with Versh, who is carrying Benjy. Jason follows sullenly behind with his hands in his pockets, while Quentin, plainly upset, lingers at the rear.

They return to find all the lights on in the house, and they are greeted by Mr Compson. Jason immediately tells their father what Quentin and Caddy did. Mr Compson, however, is not very concerned. He simply tells the children to have supper in the kitchen with the servants. At Caddy's request, Mr Compson places her in charge.

Benjy senses that something is wrong, and he begins to cry. Quentin refuses to eat. Jason eats but then begins to cry. Caddy assumes a parental role, and tells the other children to behave. Finally, Frony, daughter of Dilsey, blurts out that Damuddy, their maternal grandmother, is dead and their parents are in mourning. At this, Jason begins to weep. Caddy insists that the adults are just having a party.

Caddy goes outside and, assisted by a push from Versh, climbs a tree to look out and see if there is a funeral or a party. Benjy observes, for the first of many times in the novel, that "Caddy smelled like trees." Finally, without being able to confirm what has happened, the children are sent to the sick room to sleep. Jason cries and says he wants to sleep with Damuddy. When Dilsey threatens him with a whipping, he finally quiets down.

Quentin and Jason share one bed, while Caddy sleeps next to Benjy in another. Mr Compson comes in, kisses Caddy, and tells her to take good care of Benjy. They go to sleep.

Caddy's Wedding (1910)

When the children are walking back from the stream, they pass the barn. The association with the barn sets off the first of a series of scenes from the time of Caddy's wedding. T.P. has found an alcoholic drink he calls "sassprilluh," possibly champagne, stored in the cellar for the wedding. He is now drunk. Quentin (male), probably upset about losing Caddy, takes his anger out on T.P. with several blows. T.P., however, is not hurt at all. He does fall over repeatedly, but far more from the combination of alcohol and

laughter than the punches. Quentin then gives Benjy a drink, probably to quiet him.

Later, Benjy sees Caddy with flowers in her hair, wearing a long wedding veil. He calls to her over and over. T.P. takes Benjy away, and they both drink some more of the alcoholic beverage. Soon T.P. is too drunk to walk, and falls down in the meadow. Quentin kicks him, and Caddy comes up and puts her arms around Benjy. This time, however, Benjy goes away, he has done this in the past when Caddy wore perfume and no longer smelled like trees.

A short time later, after Caddy has left, Benjy runs after a group of young girls looking for her. At the initiative of Jason IV, he is then taken away to an institution and castrated.

The Changing of Benjamin's Name (1900)

The first reference to the changing of Benjy's name is in the quarters of the Negro servants in 1910, the year of Quentin's suicide. Roskus, the husband of Dilsey, is suffering from rheumatism and is almost incapacitated. He remarks that the retardation of Benjy, now fifteen, has been a clear sign that there is no luck in the Compson house. T.P. confirms this by saying that he and Versh have heard a screech owl the past night, a portent of Quentin's death. Roskus remarks that the changing of Benjy's name first confirmed for him that the house was shadowed by ill fortune. Dilsey tries to get Roskus to drop the subject, perhaps in part because Benjy, increasingly rejected by the Compsons, has virtually become part of the servants' household.

We are later taken back to 1900, when the family has first realized that Benjy is retarded. Caddy tells Dilsey that the name has been changed from "Maury" to "Benjamin" by Mrs Compson. The child had originally been named after the brother of Mrs Compson, but now the mother does not want him associated with her side of the family. "Benjamin," Caddy says, is a better name for the child since it comes from the Bible. Dilsey interprets the change as an attempt to ward off bad luck, and says that it will not help him. She regards her own name as so permanent that it will outlast her life and even her memory. Though Dilsey cannot read, she believes her name is written in a book in heaven. When her name is read by the angels, she will answer.

One rainy day, Caddy is carrying Benjy, but Mrs Compson tells Caddy to put him down, saying that it will ruin Caddy's aristocratic posture. Caddy replies that Benjy is not heavy, and Mrs Compson says that she fears spoiling the child. When Caddy refers to the boy as "Benjy," Mrs Compson objects, saying nicknames are only for the vulgar, and he must be referred to as "Benjamin." She orders Caddy to take a cushion away from Benjy, at which time the retarded child begins to cry inconsolably. Caddy takes Benjy to watch the fire, and the sight quiets him.

Caddy then finds that Jason IV has maliciously cut up Benjy's paper dolls. She physically attacks Jason and Mr Compson has to restrain her. Jason denies having done anything wrong, saying he thought the dolls were old pieces of paper.

Later, Versh tells Benjamin that by changing his name they are making Benjy into a "bluegum" or sorcerer. The servant tells of a black preacher who was made into a bluegum. When a woman looked him in the eye under a full moon, he could impregnate her visually. He produced many children in this way. One day, these bluegum children set upon their father in the woods and ate him, leaving the skeleton to be found by possum hunters.

Uncle Maury and Mrs Patterson (Christmas 1902)

Uncle Maury sends Benjy to deliver a letter to Mrs Patterson. Caddy helps Benjy, saying that it is a surprise for Christmas. When they arrive at the Patterson house, Caddy decides to take the letter over herself. Mrs Patterson goes to the doorway, then becomes upset and yells at Benjy. Mr Patterson, who has been chopping a Christmas tree, becomes furious. He runs over and grabs the letter. There is a lot of commotion and Benjy runs away.

Later, we learn that Uncle Maury is not well, probably as a result of having been assaulted by Mr Patterson. Uncle Maury is furious, and says he will shoot Mr Patterson. On hearing about this, Mr Compson laughs. He has no respect for Uncle Maury, who is constantly asking his sister, Mrs Compson, for money and alcohol. Mrs Compson is upset by the attack on her brother. Mr Compson replies that Uncle Maury just proves the superiority of the Compson side of the family.

Analysis

Any attempt to explicate the first part of the novel must disentangle the various chains of events. In doing this, however, we should still remember that they are entangled not simply out of confusion but for a purpose. The sort of sequence we usually call "logical" is, as modern scientists and artists have recognized, not necessarily the only valid one, and rearranging the events in this way can risk distorting them.

The changes of scene are, among other things, an attempt by Faulkner to reconstruct the way the world appears to a thirty-three-year-old retarded man. As I will explain later, the author regards this perspective as having a certain validity. It is not just a result of stupidity. We can appreciate this endeavor, as well as the poetry of Faulkner's language, without placing the events in a more sequential form. Those readers who have the interest and a little extra time at their disposal may even wish to read the section a first time without turning to this or any other explication, in order to get a better feeling for the way Benjy sees the world.

The title of the novel is taken from a famous passage spoken by the protagonist in Shakespeare's *Macbeth*, after he learns of his wife's suicide:

> Out, out, brief candle!
> Life's but a walking shadow, a poor player
> That struts and frets his hour upon the stage
> And then is heard no more: it is a tale
> Told by an idiot, full of sound and fury
> Signifying nothing.
>
> (Act V, Scene 5)

Motifs from this passage, such as the candle and the shadow are mentioned now and then throughout the novel.

The passage, however, pertains especially to the first part. This is, very literally, "a tale told by an idiot." Benjy, who is profoundly retarded, cannot actually speak, but the first section of the novel is narrated from his point of view. It is, in other words, what Benjy might say if he were able to speak.

Some critics have pointed to the words "signifying nothing" in the passage by Shakespeare as an indication that Faulkner considered the novel incapable of being interpreted. *The Sound and the Fury*, however, is full of symbolism, which certainly invites attempts at interpretation. It is probable that Faulkner intended the words "signifying nothing" to pertain especially to the first of the four parts. They describe the world of Benjy, which is full of sharp, clear sensuous images but where understanding never develops. Benjy sees and hears many things, but it never occurs to him that these impressions could actually mean or "signify" anything.

One way to understand the words of Shakespeare places Benjy, in a sense, almost in the position of God. This idea may impress some readers as blasphemous, but it is not without precedent. Throughout history, people have regarded the retarded in a wide range of different ways. At times, their silence has been interpreted as an indication of divine wisdom. When he wrote the novel, Faulkner may have been thinking partly of *The Idiot*, a famous work of fiction written by the Russian Fydor Dostoyevsky and first published in 1868. Dostoyevsky imagines Christ appearing in the late nineteenth century as somebody often taken for an "idiot."

Faulkner suggests an analogy between Benjy and Christ by making his first narrator 33 years old, the age Christ was when he was impaled. Benjy, furthermore, seems able to sense intuitively when something is wrong in a way that often appears mystical. He withdraws from Caddy, for example, after she has been promiscuous. Finally, Benjy seems, with his suffering, to take on the guilt of the Compson family in much the way Christ took on "the sins of the world."

Most significantly, God views the world, according to many cultures from the perspective of eternity. Mortals, by contrast, can only perceive the world within time. For Benjy, however, all events take place simultaneously. There is no distinction between past, present and future.

The analogies between Benjy and Christ are not very detailed. There are no clear parallels, for example, between specific events in the life of Benjy and that of Christ. Benjy also has no lessons for people, verbal or otherwise. As so often in his novels, Faulkner seems to play with Christian symbolism without developing it.

Nevertheless, Christians sometimes say that Christ is in every one of us. The suggestion that Benjy is Christ-like will at least have

the effect of raising Benjy's status for the reader. Faulkner wants us
to take him seriously as a character.

There are other ways that we can interpret the timeless character of Benjy's world. He might, for example, represent the old
South, which remains fixed in time, stubbornly resisting the pressures to modernize. Above all else, Benjy seems to crave the stability of fixed routines. Whenever familiar patterns are disrupted,
Benjy begins to cry. This, in turn, makes it more difficult for those
around Benjy to adapt to a changing world.

Change and resistance to it are already indicated by the initial
scene of the novel. The property that was once a meadow where
children played is now a golf course. This symbolizes the transition from a traditional, rural way of life to a commercial one. Benjy
cannot accept the change, and returns, accompanied by Luster,
through a hole in the fence to the scene of his childhood.

Benjy is still looking for his childhood, most especially his
sister Caddy. This quest is ironically echoed by others. The golfer is
searching for his ball, which has been picked up by Benjy. Luster is
looking for his lost quarter, which will enable him to go to a minstrel show in the evening.

The episodes about Benjy and the other Compson children are
among the subtlest in the novel. By comparison with what hap-
pens later, they seem positively idyllic. Yet, the various pathologies which will destroy them are already present. The episodes
represent, in the context of the novel, a fall from innocence into
corruption.

All of the Compson children will prove incapable of forming
loving, supportive relationships, either within the family or outside of it. Not once in the novel do any of them declare love for
another. Their emotional development is, as will be increasingly
apparent, stifled by the need to live up to traditions which have
long been virtually meaningless. The Compsons are a lineage em-
bracing governors and generals, yet their claim to greatness is tied
to an aristocratic order that is disappearing.

The line of the Bascombs, from which the children are de-
scended through their mother Caroline, is less distinguished and
even more degenerate. It will end with Maury Bascomb, the brother
of Caroline, a pathetic drunk and a philanderer who is constantly

asking for money. The pretensions to nobility only inhibit the
Compsons and Bascombs from full participation in everyday affairs. The children seem to have no companions from beyond their
estate, and only Quentin, the eldest of the Compson children, even
goes to school.

Patterns that will persist throughout the book are established
at the beginning. As we first see them by the stream, Quentin and
Caddy are just starting to enter adolescence, the age when young
people discover their sexuality. Caddy gets her dress wet and decides to take it off. Quentin, who is later obsessed with defending
Caddy's virtue, tries in vain to prevent her from removing her dress.
When he strikes Caddy and she falls, muddying her drawers, this
foreshadows her later promiscuity. As Caddy and Quentin begin
to splash one another, there is something erotic in the play.

Afterwards, the children, Quentin especially, feel strongly that
they have done something wrong. Quentin fears a whipping if
anybody tells. Corporal punishment, clearly, is usual in the
Compson family. Caddy, however, says she does not care if she gets
a whipping, and that she will, herself will tell what happened. The
entire scene, while superficially innocent, is pervaded by sugges-
tions of incest and sado-masochism.

The anticipation of punishment, however, turns out to be just
an expression of the guilt which Caddy and Quentin feel. Jason,
who stays apart from the other children tells Mr Compson what
his brother and sister have done, only to find that their father
attaches no importance to the transgression whatsoever.

The way Caddy takes off her dress at the stream probably feeds
the obsession that all three brothers will later feel for her. In every
case, there are strong hints of an erotic bond. No doubt this is partly
because the boys, isolated by the aristocratic pretensions of their
family, appear to have grown up without any other young ladies
around.

The incestuous attachment is most overt in the case of
Quentin, who later not only fantasizes about incest but will tell (or
imagine telling) his father that he and Caddy are guilty of this.
Quentin also resents any boyfriends of Caddy with all the fury of a
jilted lover. A comparable attachment is apparent with Benjy, who
has slept with Caddy until the age of thirteen (Let us remember

that retarded people generally do not lack a normal degree of sexuality).

The incestuous attachment is least apparent in the case of Jason IV. He constantly attacks and exploits Caddy at every opportunity. His enormous resentment against his sister is hard to explain if he never felt any attraction toward her. Caddy, by contrast, seems totally uninterested in Jason from the start.

The extreme bitterness of Jason toward Caddy may reflect the pain of being rejected by her. It might even have begun as a desperate attempt to shake Caddy out of her indifference and establish some sort of relationship with her.

When the children get back, Mr Compson, totally indifferent to the muddy drawers, puts Caddy in charge, despite the fact that Quentin is older. She has taken over the maternal role in the family. This is largely because Mrs Compson, the actual mother is cold and remote. She does little except complain. This leaves Caddy, however, playing a wide range of feminine roles toward each of the male members of the household. She must be simultaneously sister, mother, and wife to various members of the family. Though she is plainly flattered by her power in the family, the burden is obviously far too much for her. Furthermore, it arouses resentment on the part of her mother.

Damuddy was the maternal grandmother of the children, but we learn virtually nothing about her beyond a comment by Mrs Compson that she spoiled Jason. Perhaps her death symbolizes the final passing of the aristocratic order. At any rate, it is the children's first contact with mortality. The parents, stifled by their notions of propriety, are unable to help their children deal with the realities of either love or death. The funeral, in consequence, is kept secret from the children. Jason and Quentin, however, immediately suspect what is going on, and only Caddy attempts to deny it.

Caddy later emerges as the most caring and sensitive of the Compson children, while Jason becomes diabolical in his cruelty. Faulkner, however, was far too sophisticated a novelist to fill his works with one-dimensional heroes or villains. He delighted in exploring the paradoxes and complexities of human motivation. At the scene of Damuddy's death, those roles are reversed. Jason, overwhelmed by grief, actually comes across as the most sensitive.

Caddy, who treats the occasion as an adventure, appears charming and spirited yet rather callous.

When the children have been put to bed and Mr Compson comes in, he once again shows his insensitivity as a father. He is unable to deal with intensely emotional situations himself, much less help his children through them. It is Jason and Quentin who need comfort, yet he turns only to Caddy and Benjy. Even with Caddy, Mr Compson seems to be less offering than asking reassurance.

Had Jason been able to acknowledge and deal with his grief and isolation, he could probably have grown up to be a far more compassionate human being. Quentin, had he been helped to confront his awakening sexuality, probably would not have been ruined for normal relationships. The same might be true of Caddy, had she not had to carry such heavy emotional burdens at such an early age. Even Benjy might have been spared a good deal of grief if people had addressed the reasons for his moaning rather than simply trying to shut him up. Neither parent, however, shows any awareness of the emotional needs of their children.

The inability of the Compson parents to acknowledge or confront misfortune is shown again in the incidents surrounding the changing of Benjy's name. Mrs Compson had named the child after her brother, but, on realizing he is retarded, she wishes to banish Benjy from at least her side of the family. As on so many other occasions, her response to a problem is to look for ways in which to deny its existence.

To be named for the dissolute Maury is hardly much of a blessing, so Caddy is right to say that "Benjamin" is a better name. This, in the Bible, is the youngest son of Jacob, toward whom his father, Joseph, was especially protective, and became head of one of the ten lost tribes of Israel. Yet Roskus, the old servant, interprets the change as an attempt to deny the curse on the family. His wife Dilsey is also not pleased, for she regards a name as written in the book of heaven to be called on judgment day.

Most people take the changing of the name for an unnatural act, leaving Benjy even more ambiguous than before. According to Versh, it makes Benjy into a supernatural being known as a "bluegum," possessing the power to impregnate women with a glance by the full moon. Superstitious as the attitudes of the servants are, they express attitudes that many others share.

The name does not take entirely. The name "Benjy," which sounds somewhat like "Maury," is a sort of a compromise, saving the profoundly retarded child the trouble of having to learn to respond to an entirely new designation. As usual, Mrs Compson thinks only of her outmoded etiquette, saying that nicknames are for the vulgar. Nevertheless, even she eventually begins to use the nickname. Right after the change, Jason maliciously cuts up Benjy's paper dolls, an attempt to force him out of the protected world of childhood.

The change of name anticipates an even bigger adjustment for Benjy. The sole source of protection and stability in Benjy's life is Caddy, yet, unable to grow up himself, he does not let her grow up either. When she begins to wear perfume, a sign of entering womanhood, Benjy withdraws from her. Then, as her marriage approaches, he senses that he may lose her. When her prior pregnancy is discovered, her husband throws her out and she is banished from the Compson house. Mrs Compson, again trying to deny any misfortune, bans the use of Caddy's name in the house, making the change still more abrupt and the adjustment more difficult for Benjy.

Looking for Caddy, he runs after some young girls, and Jason and Mr Compson have Benjy castrated. People have long felt uncomfortable with the sexuality of the retarded, an attitude reflected in Versh's earlier remark about Benjy having become a bluegum. Benjy, however, has always been obviously harmless. The response supports the notion that Jason was jealous of the favors Caddy once lavished on her youngest brother.

Caddy, though we never actually learn very much about her, is more the center of the novel than any other character. She is present through her effects on other characters, most especially her brothers, but we can barely guess what she is thinking or feeling. Since just about every other major character is obsessed, in various ways, with her, she provides the dynamic force of the novel. Benjy and Quentin will hardly change at all, Jason only slightly. Caddy, by contrast, will become a young adult, then a woman and mother, a progression which disrupts the static world of her brothers and which they cannot accept.

Study Questions

1. Explain why Benjy cried when the golfer called, "Here caddie."

2. What was Luster looking for by the stream?

3. When Caddy and Benjy passed the pig pen on Christmas Eve, why did Caddy say the pigs were upset?

4. Why, as children, did Caddy and Quentin think they would be whipped?

5. Why did Caddy climb a tree?

6. What did Benjy think of Caddy after she had climbed the tree?

7. What did Uncle Maury have Benjy deliver?

8. Why was Benjy's name changed?

9. Why did Benjy withdraw from Caddy?

10. What was unusual about how the man on a swing with Miss Quentin was dressed?

Answers

1. Benjy cried because the word "caddie" was like the name of his sister who had left her home.

2. Luster was looking for a lost quarter by the stream.

3. Caddy told Benjy the pigs were upset because one of them had just been slaughtered.

4. As children, Caddy and Quentin thought they would be whipped because Quentin had knocked Caddy down and she had muddied her drawers.

5. Caddy climbed a tree to see if the adults were having a party or a funeral.

6. After Caddy had climbed a tree, Benjy thought that she smelled like trees.

7. Uncle Maury had Benjy deliver a letter to Mrs Patterson, with whom Uncle Maury was having an affair.

8. Benjy's name was changed because people realized he was retarded and, in consequence, did not want him named after Mrs Compson's brother.

9. Benjy withdrew from Caddy because she had used perfume and no longer smelled like trees.

10. The man on a swing with Miss Quentin wore a red tie.

Suggested Essay Topics

1. Faulkner in the first section of *The Sound and the Fury* represented the world of a retarded man as filled with sensuous impressions that are joined by associations. There are no abstractions. Many experts on retardation will question whether that representation applies to all the retarded. Do you know any retarded people? Do you think it applies to them?

2. Several of the characters in *The Sound and the Fury* might be characterized as insane or nearly so, but only Benjy is retarded. How do people distinguish between insanity and retardation? How well do you think these distinctions apply in the novel by Faulkner?

3. The name "Benjamin" is taken from the youngest son of Jacob in the Biblical story of Joseph (Genesis IV). Read this story and see what references you can find to it in the first part of *The Sound and the Fury.* Why do you think the name "Benjamin" or "Benjy" was chosen?

4. *The Sound and the Fury* never records any extended conversation between Caddy and her father, yet he seems to have been fond of her. He puts her, rather than her elder brother, in charge on the night of Damuddy's death. What do you think the relationship between Mr Compson and Caddy was like?

5. One thing that can make the first part of *The Sound and the Fury* confusing is that Benjy uses the name "Quentin" for both his brother and his niece and does not otherwise distinguish between them. Does Benjy fully realize that they are two different people? How much do you think he distinguishes between the name and the human being?

Part Two

Quentin: June 2, 1910

New Characters:

Dalton Ames: *the seducer of Caddy, with whom Quentin either remembers or imagines having had an encounter*

Anse: *the law enforcement officer who arrests Quentin*

Gerald Bland: *a young man from Kentucky who reminds Quentin of Dalton Ames. Quentin picks a fight with Gerald Bland and loses badly*

Mrs Bland: *the mother of Gerald Bland, who boasts about her son's sexual conquests*

Three Boys: *youngsters Quentin encounters as they gaze at an enormous trout and daydream about the prize they could win by catching it*

Deacon: *an elderly Negro man who hangs around campus and reminds Quentin of Roskus. Quentin entrusts Deacon with the suicide note to Shreve*

Herbert Head: *the groom of Caddy, who leaves her on discovering that she is pregnant*

Jeweler: *a man who examines Quentin's broken watch*

Julio: *an Italian immigrant who thinks that Quentin is trying to abduct his sister*

Little Italian Girl: *a lost girl Quentin attempts to befriend, only to be accused of abduction*

Natalie: *an early girlfriend of Quentin, who arouses the anger of Caddy*

Shreve MacKenzie: *a roommate of Quentin at Harvard (He is also a character in Faulkner's novel* Absalom, Absalom*)*

Spoade: *a fellow-student of Quentin at Harvard, who has a reputation for laziness*

The Squire: *the local official who tries Quentin for kidnapping a little girl*

Summary

The second part of *The Sound and the Fury* is narrated from the perspective of Quentin, the oldest of the Compson children. Though not as disconnected as the first part, it also moves back and forth in time and space. In one respect, it can be even more difficult than the first part, since it blends not only different events but also fantasy and reality. We cannot always separate what Quentin remembers from what he imagines. Nevertheless, everything in Part Two is centered around a continuous sequence of events.

Quentin, now a student at Harvard, begins the day on which he has planned to commit suicide. He contemplates his watch, which is an heirloom given to him by his father. It came with the advice that it is futile to try to conquer time. The watch, for his father, symbolized the futility of all human endeavor, and the illusive nature of all victory or defeat. Mr Compson presented the watch to Quentin with the words, "I give you the mausoleum of all hope and desire."

Quentin listens to the watch and meditates on the nature of time. He is briefly interrupted by his roommate, Shreve, who is getting ready for class. Then Quentin's thoughts turn to the wedding of his sister Caddy. Quentin remembers the pregnancy of his sister, which caused her new husband, Herbert Head, to abandon her. He told his father that it was not Dalton Ames, a boyfriend, that took Caddy's virginity. It was he, Quentin, who committed incest with his sister. His father responded to this, as to most everything, with cynical philosophizing.

Upset by the memories, Quentin takes the watch from the top

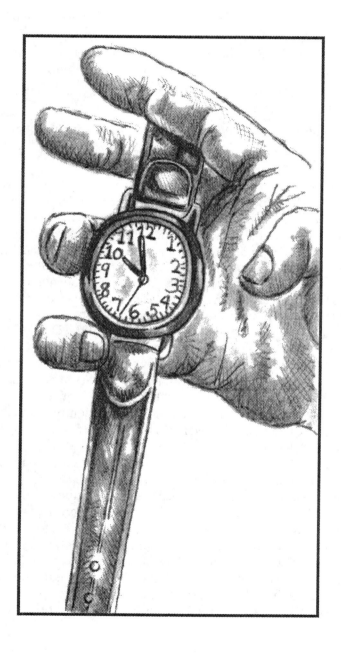

of his dresser, breaks the crystal and tears off the hands. He cuts his thumb in the process, but the watch continues to tick. Quentin puts iodine on the cut, cleans up the blood and begins meticulously putting everything in order for his suicide.

He arranges his clothes, packs his trunk, arranges a stack of books, showers and shaves. Then Quentin writes two suicide notes, one to his father and one to Shreve. He mails the first note, enclosing the key to his trunk, then entrusts the other to Deacon, an old African-American man from the South who constantly hangs around campus.

He takes the broken watch to a jeweler, who examines it. The jeweler says that the mechanism appears to be in order, but he will have to look more closely to know for sure. Quentin declines to leave the watch in the shop, saying that he does not need a timepiece at the moment. He notices the ticking of many watches and clocks all around him, and asks the jeweler if any one of them tells the correct time. In answer, the jeweler begins to tell Quentin the time. Quentin cuts him off, pleased to find that the jeweler considers the time on the timepieces to be irrelevant.

After leaving, Quentin goes to a hardware store and purchases two flat irons which he will fasten to his feet when he jumps into the Charles River. Having made the preparations to kill himself, Quentin has nothing left to do. He gets on a streetcar. The ride becomes an occasion for a long meditation, as Quentin recalls a wide range of people and events from childhood to his current life at Harvard. These center, most especially, on Caddy and his father.

Quentin thinks of how the land they called "Benjy's pasture" was sold to pay for his tuition at Harvard. Then he also thinks of his mother, who constantly complained about making sacrifices. She approved only of Jason, and thought of the other children as a judgment against her. All of these recollections are constantly interrupted by memories of his father, who was always cynical yet never cruel.

He thinks of Gerald Bland, an acquaintance at Harvard who reminds him of Dalton Ames, the seducer of Caddy. Both speak scornfully of women and neither had a sister. Then he thinks of Herbert Head, who was to marry Caddy.

Quentin had accused Herbert Head of dishonesty, but Caddy interrupted and told Quentin to drop the matter. She did not care

greatly whether Herbert Head was honest or not. He had promised to help the family, most especially to give Jason a job at his bank. He had offered money to Quentin, who took that as an insult and refused.

Quentin thinks of how Caddy went through a period of promiscuity. Caddy, trying to hide her pregnancy, had told Quentin that she was sick. She asked him to look after Benjy and their father, anticipating that she would soon have to leave. Not comprehending what was going on, Quentin had given her his promise.

Finally, Quentin gets off the streetcar and follows a country road. Quentin hides the flat irons by the river, then walks down the road and continues his meditations. He remembers how Caddy said that she had to marry somebody. Then he imagines his suicide, and wonders how he will rise from the river at Judgment Day.

Quentin thinks of how his father, unlike his mother and himself, received the news of Caddy's pregnancy calmly. Mr Compson said that Quentin cared about virginity because he, the eldest son, was a virgin. But purity, his father continued, was unnatural. Mr Compson denied his son even the consolation of tragic destiny. Tragedy, the father said, was only experienced by spectators at second hand.

By a bridge over a stream, Quentin finds three boys with fishing poles. The boys are staring at a huge trout. They know the fish well. People have been trying, they say, to catch the trout for twenty-five years. A store in Boston had offered an expensive fishing pole to anyone who succeeded. One boy dreams of winning, while the others tease him. Quentin chats with the boys a while, shows them his watch, and advises them not to catch the old trout, who deserves to live. The boys decide the attempt to catch the fish is futile anyway, and they go to swim in another pond by a mill.

Quentin again sinks back into his memories, recalling his father's drinking himself nearly to death. The young man remembers how he and Caddy had talked of taking Benjy and going away together. They did not, in part because the pasture had been sold to pay for his tuition to Harvard, so Quentin was bound by duty to complete the term.

Coming to a bakery, Quentin sees a little Italian girl with a dirty face and pigtails by the counter. The woman in the shop speaks

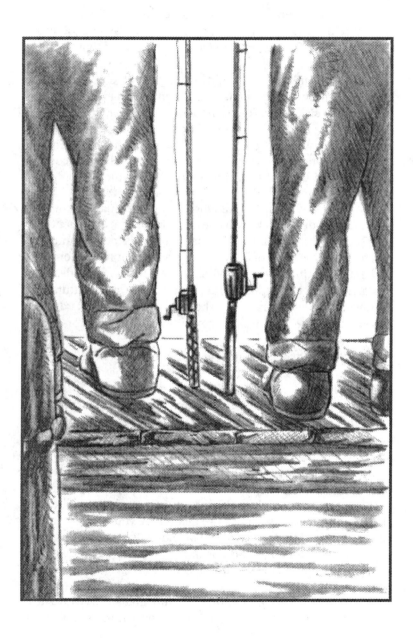

contemptuously of the child, but Quentin defends the girl and buys her a bun. On leaving, the girl, who is lost and does not speak English, tags along with Quentin.

He wants to help her find her way home, but she is unable to tell him where she lives. Quentin thinks again of the comments of his father, who viewed women as delicate and mysterious yet filled with filth. He and the girl come to a mill, where three boys are swimming. They suggest that Quentin bring the girl to Anse, the town marshal. Quentin agrees, and starts to take the girl in the direction of town.

As he searches for the girl's home, Quentin thinks of Natalie, an early girlfriend of his, of whom Caddy disapproved. Though Quentin felt his relationship with Natalie was very innocent, his sister slapped him. Caddy, Quentin thinks, is possessive toward him in much the way he is toward her.

The search for the girl's home leads Quentin back to the boys. Like many in the town, they are scornful of foreigners. This time the boys rudely tell Quentin and the girl to go away, and splash them.

As the two retreat, they are stopped by two men: Anse, the sheriff, and Julio, brother of the young girl. Julio strikes Quentin, whom he believes has been abducting his sister. The brother is extremely possessive and even threatens to kill Quentin. Anse arrests Quentin, but threatens Julio, whom he views as a contemptible foreigner.

As Anse takes Quentin into town, they meet Mrs Bland, Gerald, Shreve and Spoade with some girls. Mrs Bland and the company argue with the sheriff. Meanwhile, the little girl looks at Quentin with sympathy, until Julio shouts that he will beat her.

Anse takes Julio and Quentin, together with Quentin's acquaintances, into a courthouse, where the squire presides over a process. After hearing brief accounts of what happened from Quentin and Anse, he renders a verdict. Quentin must pay one dollar to Julio for the time lost from work and six dollars to Anse for the time spent on the case.

As they leave the courthouse, Spoade insists that Quentin was guilty of abduction. Shreve believes him to be innocent. Mrs Bland, however, is unconcerned, and she impatiently dismisses the discussion. The conversation grows increasingly trivial.

Quentin's mind goes back to his relationship with his sister Caddy. He had asked her how many men she had gone to bed with. She said only that it was "too many." Quentin then asked Caddy if she had loved them. She replied that their touch revolted her.

One day, Quentin had found Caddy by a stream. She had just gone to bed with a man, and Benjy had withdrawn from her. She was letting the water run over her thighs, trying to purify herself. Quentin asked if the man had raped her. She replied that he had not. She hated the man, yet she would still go through with it again, as she had many times before.

Caddy had asked Quentin whether he was a virgin, and he had lied that he had sex with many girls. Then he had broken down crying. Caddy had tried to comfort him. Quentin reminded Caddy of the night when Damuddy died and how Caddy dirtied her drawers.

Quentin had offered Caddy a suicide pact. He had held a knife to her throat, saying that he would slit it and then his own, Caddy had agreed. Quentin, however, had been unable to go through with the act. Instead, he had thought again of that fateful day when Damuddy died, and he began crying once more. Caddy had tried to comfort him, but Quentin was unable to stop.

After the ride, Gerald Bland begins boasting of his sexual conquests. Quentin thinks of Caddy, then picks a fight with Gerald Bland. The eldest Compson is barely able to get in a single blow. Gerald Bland, an amateur boxer, soon leaves Quentin lying on the ground, covered with blood. As Quentin regains consciousness, his mind goes back to a similar incident on the Compson estate.

Quentin remembers, or else imagines, how, a few days after the broken suicide pact, he had threatened Dalton Ames, a lover of Caddy, with death if he did not leave town immediately. Dalton Ames had looked at Quentin calmly, a cigarette in his mouth, and said that all women are bitches anyway. When Quentin tried to strike Dalton Ames, Caddy's lover caught her brother's hands. Holding both of Quentin's wrists with one hand, Dalton Ames had taken out a pistol with the other hand and, without aiming, shot a piece of bark floating in the river. Then Dalton Ames handed the gun to Quentin, who fainted on the spot.

Shreve and Spoade help Quentin up and clean off the blood. Quentin is unable to remember what just happened, and his two

young acquaintances have to explain the events. Shreve, who shares some of Quentin's disgust with Gerald Bland, offers sympathy. Spoade is irritated and a bit contemptuous. After giving Shreve and Spoade an apology for Mrs Bland, Quentin goes back to the streetcar.

On the ride back, he meditates on the reflections and shadows in the river. As the end of Quentin's life approaches, the memories, especially those of early childhood, grow even more poignant and more disconnected. He wishes for a mother to whom he could have turned for comfort. He thinks of Benjy watching himself in the mirror. He recalls how his father had called Harvard a "fine sound," worth the price of Benjy's pasture. Mr Compson then told Quentin that his mother's dream, since Quentin was born, was that her son would attend that illustrious school. Quentin also remembers admitting to his father that he had not committed incest with Caddy. His father advised him to take a vacation and forget his pain.

The painful memories do not distract Quentin from meticulous preparations for his death. He leaves his watch, still ticking, in Shreve's drawer as a gift. Then Quentin brushes his teeth and, borrowing a clothes brush from Shreve, cleans his hat. Finally, he goes out to end his life.

Analysis

Quentin is far more articulate in the expression of his feelings than either of his brothers, and the section narrated from his point of view is both the most passionate and the most intellectual. While we can generally accept the veracity of what Benjy reports, fragmentary as it is, we are never sure whether Quentin's reports are accurate. Benjy had almost no capacity for fantasy. Quentin's imagination, by contrast, is very active, and he often seems to confuse fantasy with fact. One example is when he claims to have committed incest with Caddy. Another example is when he fails to remember the fight with Gerald Bland. Nevertheless, it may be unimportant how much of what Quentin narrates is true. The truth that is most important for him is more psychological than factual. He feels guilty of incest with Caddy, for example, whether or not he actually engaged in it.

While Benjy was caught in a world outside time, Quentin is

constantly trying to escape the tyranny of time. He attempts to understand time, and, when that proves impossible, he tries to destroy time. This is symbolized by the breaking of the watch his father gave him. It proves futile, since the watch simply goes on ticking even without its hands. The impulse culminates in suicide, which is his attempt to move beyond this world to eternity.

He is especially obsessed with his sister and father, but his pathology is intertwined with the lives of his whole family. He is the romantic, the one who constantly tries to uphold an ideal of absolute purity in the confrontation with the corruption all around him. Caddy rebels against her family through promiscuity, while Quentin rebels by maintaining his virginity, yet the two are profoundly similar in other areas.

There is a reversal of traditional roles, since, as Quentin notes early in the section, men in the South are not traditionally expected to be virgins and lie about it when they are. The reverse tends to be the case with women. Caddy does not enjoy her affairs with men, yet she indulges in them largely in reaction to the stifling and outmoded notions of propriety upheld by Mrs Compson. In a parallel way, Quentin reacts against the cynical comments of his father, who constantly seeks to refute any ideal of virtue and nobility.

Seeking to affirm his values, Quentin constantly does the opposite of what his father suggests. Mr Compson gives Quentin the watch so that he will forget about time, and Quentin reacts by becoming obsessed with time. Mr Compson tells Quentin to forget the past, and the son becomes constantly preoccupied with memories.

The members of the Compson family all feed their collective pathologies. The cynicism of Mr Compson is, like the promiscuity of Caddy, at least partly a reaction against his wife's rigid notions of appropriate behavior. Trapped by family tradition and by loveless marriage, he views his personal despair as a universal condition. Since Mr Compson himself cannot live for noble ideals, he prefers to view these values as absurd.

It is relatively easy for him to be nihilistic, however, since his position protects him from the consequences of his ideas. The counsel of despair is usually expressed in a very old-fashioned, florid sort of language. This suggests that Mr Compson may have been more interested in eloquence than in content. He drinks heavily, but his destructive impulses are otherwise purely intellectual. While he insists that nothing matters, his behavior, apart from the alcoholism, is totally conventional. He never openly violates societal expectations. He lives by fixed patterns. His irresponsible talk is a compensation for a lack of personal freedom.

There is no sign of cruelty in Mr Compson. The man is simply melancholy. He seems to genuinely wish to support his children, and he has no notion of the devastating effect his statements have. His children, however, must overcome this nihilism if they hope to have normal, healthy lives, something they fail to do.

Mrs Compson, for her part, has doubtless become more rigid and narrow-minded in reaction to the despairing talk of her husband. Though she may think that she is affirming old values, her talk centers only on arbitrary rules. For her, everything is reduced to empty social forms, which no longer are supported either by religion or by any other living tradition. In her way, Mrs Compson is as nihilistic as her husband, and most readers find her even less sympathetic. Nevertheless, the book is full of hints of frustrated attempts at tenderness between her, her children and her husband.

Mr Compson sometimes makes snide remarks on the superiority of his genealogy. The Bascombs, the maternal side of the family, are headed by the drunken, impoverished Uncle Maury. Mrs Compson, intimidated by the distinguished lineage of her husband, constantly feels the need to defend her own line. This creates a sort of rivalry within the household. The mother claims only Jason, whom she prefers, for her own side, and rejects the others as part of her husband's heritage.

To a great extent, the nihilism of the Compsons and Bascombs is an indirect legacy of slavery. The social order remains based on patterns established under slavery, even though that institution has long been discredited and abolished. The Negroes continue to live in separate quarters, and serve in the ancestral Compson house as servants. These ways are perpetuated not out of any profound conviction, but out of social inertia. People, black and white, care for order and stability more than reason. Unable to justify their way of life, however, people find that all their values are precarious.

Quentin, in going to Harvard, leaves his ancestral home far behind. He is highly uncomfortable in Cambridge. Like the little Italian girl and her brother, he is something of a "foreigner." Without the restraining power of the rigid social expectations of home, he sees the full destructive power of his father's nihilism. People like Gerald Ames seem to live the nihilism that his father merely preached. While Mr Compson associated women with filth, Gerald treats them like dirt.

Furthermore, the education of Quentin at Harvard is for no purpose, either practical or spiritual, beyond maintaining the social pretensions of the family. Quentin has not so far as we learn, expressed any desire to go there. His father calls Harvard "a fine sound," in other words, a status symbol. Mrs Compson, Quentin's father tells him, dreamed since his birth that her eldest son would go to Harvard. Attending the school is one more social symbol designed to bolster the status of a declining family. Furthermore, Quentin constantly feels guilty because "Benjy's pasture" was sold to pay for his education and his father's drinking habit. The only positive note is that Quentin postpones his suicide until the end of the semester so the money will not be wasted. That, however, is merely one more concession to social forms.

The tyranny of social codes is demonstrated by Quentin's meticulous attention to formalities as he prepares to kill himself. He arranges and packs his belongings carefully. Having done this, and having also arranged for delivery of two suicide notes, he has one day of nearly complete freedom. Nothing Quentin does now can change him, yet there are no final dreams or pleasures which he chooses to pursue. Instead, he wanders aimlessly.

Quentin identifies with the huge trout in the pond that has driven all the others away, and tells the boys they ought to leave the fish in peace. This trout, according to the three boys, for twenty-five years represents a traditional order which is doomed. Though it can still intimidate the boys, a reward has been placed on the creature's head. The fish can only wait in splendid isolation as it grows weak and finally succumbs.

When Quentin tries to befriend the little girl, he sees how dangerous possessiveness can be. Julio, her brother, tries to protect the child with the same fanaticism Quentin feels toward Caddy.

But an accident has turned Julio, a man who might have understood Quentin, into an adversary. Even more ironically, he is rescued by a party led by Gerald Bland and his mother, who scorn the values Quentin wishes to uphold.

Mrs Bland supports male domination, but she dominates the young men. Like Quentin, she is from the South and has strong aristocratic pretensions, but they are expressed by cultivating the most brutal and coarse aspects of the nobility. She may well be capable of believing that Quentin is guilty of abducting the young girl and seeing it as a demonstration of his manliness. The young ladies in the car seem to regard her and her son with a combination of horror and fascination.

Just about every young female reminds Quentin of Caddy. The confrontation with Gerald, at any rate, makes Quentin think of Dalton Ames, who seduced his sister. But the scene of the confrontation between Quentin and Dalton Ames, coherent yet very strange, is more like a hallucination than a memory.

Dalton Ames is a caricature. He appears to be extremely self-assured, suave, wealthy and expert with weapons. He has a predatory attitude toward women. Readers today will think of James Bond, but such figures were a standard feature of cheap adventure stories long before that British secret agent was invented.

The final day of Quentin's life has been a series of misunderstandings, defeats and humiliations. As his actual death approaches, the impressions in Quentin's mind become more wild and disconnected, while his actions become more methodical and careful. When he places the watch in Shreve's dresser, it is a way of passing on a heritage to the person at Harvard who understood him best. His final acts of cleaning up suggest, however, that even his suicide is no deed of transcendent passion. Even in death, mundane concerns with appearances take precedence above all else.

The narrative seems abruptly cut off at the end. The account of the day cannot possibly be complete without Quentin's drowning. Everything has prepared us for that. Such an obvious omission could not possibly be accidental. The conclusion is a deliberate anticlimax.

There are a number of possible reasons for this omission. Perhaps the conclusion was intended to confirm the statement of

Quentin's father that tragedy is impossible since it is experienced "second hand." What Mr Compson meant was that tragedy is something felt by an audience at the theater, not the defeated hero himself. By denying Quentin an audience, the author may deprive his gesture in committing suicide of meaning.

Another possibility is that leaving the section of the novel unfinished was a way of respecting Quentin's solitude. There is something rather invasive, even presumptuous, in the literary technique used here by Faulkner, which is known as "stream of consciousness." This technique attempts to record the most intimate thoughts of a protagonist. Perhaps it was as a gesture of respect for Quentin that Faulkner allowed him the full solitude during his final moments.

It could also be that Faulkner meant to acknowledge that the novel was incapable of completion. On a number of occasions, he called *The Sound and the Fury* his "most splendid failure." Great literary works, he believed, began with ideas too magnificent to ever be fully realized, but were moving precisely because they aimed at the impossible.

Study Questions

1. What did Quentin do with the watch from his father?

2. What, for Quentin, was the significance of the month of June?

3. What did Quentin tell his father that he and Caddy had done?

4. What did Quentin enclose with the suicide note to his father?

5. How did the Compson family pay for Quentin's tuition to Harvard?

6. What reward did a store in Boston offer to anybody who could catch the giant trout?

7. Where did the three boys go after they gave up the idea of catching the trout?

8. What did Caddy do to Natalie, the girlfriend of Quentin?

9. What did Dalton Ames do with his gun after he had demonstrated how it worked?

10. What is the last thing that Quentin does before going out to commit suicide?

Answers

1. Quentin broke the glass of the watch, then tore off the hands.

2. Quentin called June "the month of brides," thinking of the wedding of his sister Caddy.

3. Quentin told his father that he and Caddy had committed incest.

4. Quentin enclosed the key to his trunk with the suicide note to his father.

5. The Compson family paid for Quentin's tuition to Harvard by selling the piece of land known as "Benjy's pasture."

6. A store in Boston offered a fishing pole worth $25 to anyone who could catch the giant trout.

7. After they gave up the idea of catching the trout, the three boys went to a mill pond to swim.

8. Caddy pushed Natalie down a ladder.

9. After he had demonstrated how it worked, Dalton Ames offered his gun to Quentin.

10. The last thing Quentin does before going out to commit suicide is to borrow a brush from Shreve and clean his hat.

Suggested Essay Topics

1. Discuss the significance of Quentin's heirloom watch in *The Sound and the Fury.* Why does Mr Compson call it "the mausoleum of all hope and desire?" Why does Quentin break the watch? Why does Quentin take it to the jeweler, if he does not really want the watch repaired? Why does he finally leave the watch in the drawer of Shreve MacKenzie? To appreciate the significance of the symbol, it may help to remember that watches, when the story was written were generally larger and more ornate than those used today. They ticked far more loudly, and had to be wound regularly.

2. The section narrated from Quentin's point of view blends not only past and present but fantasy and reality. How much of what Quentin reports actually happened and how much do you think he imagined? Do you think, for example, that the confrontation with Dalton Ames actually took place or not? If it did, do you think it happened as Quentin recalls it?

3. What does Quentin mean when he speaks of "little sister death?" Does this suggest that his obsession with Caddy is, in some way, an infatuation with death? Is he, in other words, in love with death? Does the association tell us anything about the way Quentin regards Caddy?

4. Quentin is terrified of his own sexuality, in part because it is incestuously focused on his sister Caddy. Do you believe a psychologist would have been able to help him? If so, do you think he would have wanted the help?

5. *The Sound and the Fury* certainly does not give us a very attractive picture of the South, but the depiction of the North is just as harsh. While the South is especially marked by cruelty and narrow-mindedness, the North is filled with greed and corruption. Compare in detail the people from the North and South. Which region, if any, do you think that Faulkner prefers?

Part Three

Jason: April 6, 1928

New Characters:

Earl: *owner of the department store where Jason works*

Job: *a Negro who works alongside Jason*

Lorraine: *a prostitute Jason sees in Memphis, to whom he gives money*

Summary

This part takes place on the day before that of the first part. It is narrated from the point of view of Jason, the second youngest Compson child. This part of the novel is certainly more coherent than the previous two, but we should not assume the accounts in it are necessarily more reliable. While Benjy is limited by retardation and Quentin has a tendency to fantasize, Jason's perspective is shaped by his anger and resentment.

As the section begins, Mrs Compson has just learned that Miss Quentin, her granddaughter, has been cutting school. The child told her grandmother that report cards were no longer being used, and then she forged Mrs Compson's signature. Jason responds sarcastically. Mrs Compson begins weeping, and says that Jason is the only one in the family who has not been a curse for her.

Jason offers to take over the discipline of Miss Quentin, and Mrs Compson reluctantly agrees. He goes into the kitchen, where

he finds Miss Quentin with Dilsey. As Jason starts to take off his belt to beat Miss Quentin, Dilsey grabs his arm. He threatens to strike Dilsey, but Mrs Compson appears in the door and intervenes.

Upon leaving, Jason encounters Miss Quentin again in the garage by the street. He begins to lecture her about the missing school book which, Jason claims, he paid for. Miss Quentin replies that she is certain her mother paid not only for the books but for her clothes and everything else as well. Then, to show her contempt for Jason and his money, she begins to tear off her dress in the street. Jason rushes up to stop her, and they get into a bitter argument.

Finally, when Jason arrives at the department store, Earl, his boss, directs him to help an elderly negro employee named Job to unload crates. Jason berates Job about slowness, but his colleague is unconcerned. Nobody in town seems to take Jason or his tantrums very seriously.

Jason picks up his mail from the post office, and reads a letter from Caddy. She is asking for assurance that Miss Quentin got an Easter dress and complains about her letters to Miss Quentin going unanswered. She adds that if she does not hear from Jason in the next few days she will go into town herself.

Jason goes to the telegraph office and does a little speculative investing in cotton futures. Then he opens a letter from Lorraine, his mistress in Memphis, he considers how he gave her $40 at their last meeting. Then Jason tears up the letter, since he wishes to keep his visits to Lorraine secret.

This, as we will see increasingly, is what Jason is like on the job. Almost all his time on the job during the day will be spent hanging about, making conversation and drifting from one personal matter to another. He will constantly be visiting the post office, to learn about his investments (which are always losing money). Only occasionally will he make the token gesture of waiting on a customer or attending to some other task.

We learn more about the circumstances of the Compson family through a series of flashbacks. When Caddy was abandoned by her husband, Mrs Compson prohibited the use of her name in the house. Mrs Compson wanted Miss Quentin to grow up ignorant of her mother's disgrace.

Shortly afterwards, Mr Compson died of alcoholism. Jason met

Caddy after the funeral at their father's grave. She offered Jason $100 to let her see Miss Quentin. Jason took the money and promised to fulfill his part of the bargain. A while later he drove by Caddy in a carriage, and held up the infant for her to see.

It proved hard to banish Caddy's memory from the house. To make sure Caddy did not get around him through Dilsey, Jason told Dilsey she could give Miss Quentin or Benjy leprosy just by looking at them. A few days later, however, he saw Benjy screaming and caressing Caddy's slipper, so he decided his precaution had been in vain.

Jason met again with Caddy. He told his sister that if she went to Dilsey again, Mrs Compson would fire Dilsey and send Benjy to a lunatic asylum. Caddy agreed to send checks for Miss Quentin, even though she was not allowed to see her daughter. Caddy, however, insisted that the checks be made out to Mrs Compson rather than Jason, since she had learned not to trust her youngest brother.

Jason proceeded to obtain power of attorney from his mother, saying he would deposit his checks in her account. He persuaded her to burn the checks from Caddy. He then deposited the checks for Miss Quentin, using the power of attorney, and told Mrs Compson they were his wages. Since her eyesight was poor, she failed to see through the deception. Jason burned fake checks, telling his mother they were from Caddy. He then cashed his own checks, hoarding whatever he failed to spend in a box in his room.

Moving back into the present, Jason intercepts a telegram to Miss Quentin from Caddy with a money order, rather than a check, for fifty dollars. The money order is, furthermore, made out to Miss Quentin herself. A while later, Miss Quentin comes into the office looking for her telegram. Since there is no other way to cash the check, Jason tells Miss Quentin it is a gift to her for $10 but she must sign to receive it. He then presents the money order for her to sign, while concealing the amount. Miss Quentin is very suspicious, but she eventually signs, leaving Jason to pocket $40.

Jason returns home, and presents his mother with a forged check that he says Caddy has sent for Miss Quentin. This time, however, Mrs Compson wants to accept the check rather than burn it. Jason says that since, over the years, Mrs Compson has burned

checks totaling fifty thousand dollars, she cannot start accepting them now. Finally, Mrs Compson complies and burns the check. Then Jason goes to the bank, and deposits both Caddy's usual check and the money order for Quentin. His troubles, however, are just beginning.

The next stop is the department store, where Earl has been getting frustrated with Jason's constant absence from work. Earl tells Jason that he keeps him on now only out of regard for Mrs Compson. Furthermore, Earl expresses suspicions about Jason's financial dealings. He knows that Jason has his mother's power of attorney, and he wonders how Jason bought his car. He is aware that Mrs Compson gave Jason a thousand dollars to invest in the department store, and wonders what happened to the money.

Leaving the store, Jason sees Miss Quentin with the travelling performer who wears a red tie. He tries to follow them, but the minstrel show is going to start soon, and they are soon lost in the crowd. After a bit more shuttling back and forth, Jason drives by Miss Quentin who is still with the entertainer, this time together in a car. Once again, he tries to follow them without success.

Finally, Jason returns home, exhausted after chasing around all day, and despondent over his losses on the stock market. Luster reports to him that Miss Quentin has come home and that Mrs Compson has been arguing with Dilsey. As soon as she is mentioned, Dilsey comes down and asks that Jason and Mrs Compson allow her to handle Miss Quentin.

Luster asks Jason for a quarter to see the travelling show. Jason takes out two tickets that Earl gave him the previous day and offers them to Luster for a nickel. When Luster replies that he has no nickel, Jason immediately burns the tickets.

Finally, amid increasingly bitter arguments, Jason, Miss Quentin and Mrs Compson eat dinner together. Tension in the house is approaching a breaking point. Miss Quentin suddenly runs out, slamming the door. As they finish the evening, even the relations between Jason and Mrs Compson are strained.

Analysis

Benjy longed for stability and Quentin for ideals, but rage is the driving passion for Jason. He lashes out, verbally and some-

times even physically, at nearly everybody he encounters. His cruelty is so pointless, for example when he burns tickets to the show rather than give them to Luster for free, that he impresses some readers as positively satanic. It is very easy to imagine Jason in some sort of hate organization, such as the Klu-Klux-Klan or Nazi party, participating in the most vicious crimes.

Our revulsion, however, is sometimes mixed with enjoyment at his ready wit. Even when nearly overpowered by rage and despair, he almost always seems to come out with a wisecrack. He remarks, for example, about the distinguished Compson family, "Blood... governors and generals. It's a damn good thing we never had any kings and presidents; we'd all be down there at Jackson (the state mental hospital) chasing butterflies." The comedy can be a relief after the solemn intensity of the two previous sections. It is, nevertheless, often hard to say whether we are laughing with Jason or at him.

It may partially explain, though not excuse, Jason's cruelty, if we consider the pressures he confronts. They would certainly be enough to test the decency, not to mention the sanity, of people far stronger and more capable than he. With no skills or education, he must keep up an entire mansion including its servants, and a retarded brother.

He was not raised to work, since that was not the expectation among aristocrats. His father and his Uncle Maury both turned to alcohol, rather than consider seriously how they might support their families. Jason also thinks, with some degree of justice, that Quentin and Caddy have squandered his patrimony.

As a businessman, Jason is marginally competent at best. Through carelessness, he loses money speculating on cotton. He constantly alienates anybody who might be in a position to help him. As an employee, he is virtually useless. Most of his work day is spent lounging about and reading letters. He is not good at saving money. Lorraine, a prostitute he visits, seems to have little trouble getting money out of him. Jason, in fact, does not appear even to have been successful in fooling anybody, except Mrs Compson, with his tricks. Nearly everybody else, including Earl and the sheriff, has a pretty good idea of what he is up to. If Jason is an embodiment of evil, he is a rather ridiculous one.

As the section begins, Jason finds himself in a rather menial job, working alongside and waiting on the sort of people who once would have been servants in the Compson house. The wages might be enough to live on but they are too meager to support his family's aristocratic pretensions. Unlike his father, however, he has at least made some attempt to live up his responsibilities.

Faulkner himself spoke of Jason in a way that included at least a trace of affection. The author may, indeed, have identified with Jason a bit. Literature, after all, is traditionally a rather aristocratic vocation. Faulkner had taken on menial jobs such as shoveling coal to support his pretensions to literary excellence.

This is not to say that Faulkner either accepted or condoned Jason's cruelty, but that Faulkner had a sense of humor about human foibles, his own very much included. Jason is probably something of a satiric self-portrait.

We should also be careful about dismissing Mrs Compson as simply, in Jason's words from the final section of the novel, "an old fool." Although the way she talks constantly about her own suffering certainly puts people off, her tragedy is genuine. She does defend Miss Quentin and others from the cruelty of Jason.

The self-centered whining of Mrs Compson is a response to the lack of concern and respect that others show for her. To a great extent, that lack of concern may be her own fault. While she constantly tries to solicit pity, she is unable to accept it when it comes. It is interesting that the only person in the family she has much regard for is Jason, who is totally incapable of giving the compassion she appears to crave.

There is a similar contradiction in Mrs Compson's attitude toward her husband's heritage. She is fanatically concerned about what she thinks are the forms and manners of aristocracy, even when they seem to stifle normal human relationships. She says for example, in Part One of the novel, that nicknames are only for the vulgar. At the same time, she blames all of the problems in the family on its very aristocratic heritage. No doubt in reaction to her husband, she constantly insists on the superiority of the modest Bascomb line over the Compson branch of the family tree. Like others in the family, Mrs Compson is the prisoner of a heritage that she can no longer trust.

The name of "Caddy" may be banned from the Compson household, but the name of her drowned brother lives on. It has been given to the grandchild of Mrs Compson. When somebody refers to "Quentin" it is sometimes a little hard to tell which person is referred to. The naming is appropriate. Mr Quentin appeared a bit feminine, while Miss Quentin has a somewhat masculine attitude. Benjy may not even distinguish clearly between the two.

Except perhaps for Jason, everybody in the Compson household attaches a great deal of importance to names. It is noteworthy the Mrs Compson, who changed Benjy's original name and banned Caddy's, never attempts to change that of Miss Quentin, despite the suicide of her son.

Miss Quentin has many of her mother's attributes. Like Caddy in the early years, she is rebellious. Nobody can contain or control her. Furthermore, like Caddy, she is adept at climbing trees. She has, however, been too brutalized to develop any of the gentleness of her mother.

Mrs Compson and Jason both blame the absent siblings for the financial troubles of the family. That blame is now transferred to Miss Quentin, who reminds them very strongly of both Caddy and Mr Quentin. This is, in large part, the reason Miss Quentin is treated so badly. The identification also makes it nearly impossible for Miss Quentin to develop a fully autonomous personality.

The section is so fast-paced and entertaining that we can easily overlook many puzzling aspects of the plot. Caddy, apparently, is able to send about fifty thousand dollars for the care of Miss Quentin, but we are not told how she got it. The most likely possibility is that she married a rich man.

For all we know, Caddy may still be married to Herbert Head. We learn that Herbert Head abandoned his wife, but we do not know if the separation was temporary or if it ended in divorce. It could even be that the separation was not the reason why Herbert Head failed to give Jason a job at the bank. Given what we know about Jason as both a financial manager and an employee, the idea of him working at the local bank would be enough to make anybody shudder. He would be little help to customers. Furthermore, he might embezzle large sums of money, then lose them gambling on the stock market.

If Caddy has so much money and cares so much about her daughter, why has Caddy never tried to obtain custody? Mrs Compson certainly does not seem to have much attachment to Miss Quentin. Jason, apart from the money he swindles from his niece, would be delighted to be rid of her. Could it be that Caddy must keep the daughter secret from her husband? There is no hint of such a reason. If, however, it were so, how could Caddy have sent such sums of money without her husband knowing? Even if she was not in a position to care for the child, Caddy certainly could have used the money to find Quentin a better home than the Compson estate.

Finally, there are changes in Caddy that are difficult to account for. After being so spirited as a child and young woman, why is she so passive now? Why does she constantly let herself be fooled, ordered around and easily manipulated by Jason for over fifteen years? And why, after showing such devotion to her retarded brother earlier, does she not express more concern for Benjy?

These are just a few of the puzzling aspects of the plot. Why is it that Mrs Compson is unable to read checks, yet she has no trouble reading a letter from Uncle Maury? Perhaps it might be possible, though far from easy, to invent some chain of events that would resolve all the apparent gaps and inconsistencies in the story. Generally, however, the reader is expected to accept these puzzling events without much questioning.

They do, perhaps, make sense in a thematic way. For all her brothers, Caddy is less a human being than a sort of mystical figure. She embodies a vast, and often contradictory, range of feminine roles. Almost simultaneously, she can come across as nurturer, whore, madonna and companion. She is the major focus in the lives of all her brothers: the source of protection and stability for Benjy; the image of both purity and forbidden sexuality for Quentin; the means to, apparently nearly, unlimited funds for Jason.

But who is Caddy in reality? She is far less an individual than a focus of various fantasies, specifically male fantasies, about women. In the appendix to *The Sound and the Fury* which Faulkner wrote for *The Portable Faulkner*, edited by Malcolm Crowley (1946), Caddy becomes more mysterious than ever. Vaguely associated with Nazis and with Hollywood, she journeys to great capitals across the globe.

One personality can, indeed have many facets, but the various roles that Caddy plays do not seem to be connected. It is a testimony to the narrative skill of Faulkner that he can make the plot, despite a great number of flaws, at least seem reasonably coherent.

Study Questions

1. Why did a teacher from Miss Quentin's school call Mrs Compson?

2. What did Caddy say she would do if Jason did not reply to her letter by April 10th?

3. What was Jason investing money in?

4. Why, especially, did Jason hold a grudge against Caddy?

5. How does Jason let Caddy see her infant daughter?

6. How does Jason manage to obtain the money that Caddy sends for the care of Miss Quentin?

7. What does Uncle Maury request of Jason in his letter?

8. What does Jason do when he sees Miss Quentin in a car with a travelling entertainer?

9. What does Jason learn every time he goes into the telegraph office?

10. What does Mrs Compson think Miss Quentin has been doing in her room at night?

Answers

1. A teacher from Miss Quentin's school said Mrs Compson's granddaughter had been absent far too much and was close to being expelled.

2. Caddy said that if Jason did not reply to her letter by April 10th, she would come down herself and see that her money was used to buy Miss Quentin an Easter dress.

3. Jason was investing money in cotton.

4. Jason held a grudge against Caddy, especially, because her husband, Herbert Head, had promised Jason a job at his bank but failed to make good on his pledge.

5. Jason passes Caddy in a carriage and holds up her infant daughter for her to see.

6. The checks that Caddy sends for the care of Miss Quentin are made out to Mrs Compson. Jason obtains power of attorney from Mrs Compson, cashes the checks and keeps the money.

7. Uncle Maury requests that Jason give him money from Mrs Bascomb's account, allegedly for an investment.

8. When Jason sees Miss Quentin in a car with a travelling entertainer, he tries to follow them.

9. Every time he goes into the telegraph office, Jason learns that his investments have lost more money.

10. Mrs Compson thinks Miss Quentin has been studying in her room late at night.

Suggested Essay Topics

1. All of the Compsons except Jason seem to have a rather casual attitude toward money. Why, then, is Jason obsessed with it?

2. One theme of *The Sound and the Fury* is how the commercial culture of the North is replacing traditional Southern ways. How can this change be observed in the town of Jefferson? Do you think Faulkner considered the change good or bad?

3. Caddy attempts to care for her daughter at a distance, sending money instead of giving personal affection. How does this mirror the earlier relationship between Mrs Compson and Caddy? Compare these two mother-daughter pairs.

Part Four

Dilsey: April 8, 1928

New Characters:

Old Man: *a member of the troop of travelling entertainers. When Jason presses him for information about the location of Miss Quentin, the man goes after Jason with an axe*

Troop Manager: *helps rescue Jason, then assures him that the couple he seeks is not around*

The Sheriff of Jefferson: *the law enforcement officer to whom Jason complains after Miss Quentin has taken money from his room and run away. He declines to pursue Miss Quentin*

Summary

This part of the novel is not narrated from the perspective of any character, but it centers largely around Dilsey. It takes place on Easter Sunday. Luster, to whom Dilsey gave a quarter so he could go to the show, has overslept. Mrs Compson calls Dilsey. The mistress of the house is used to sounds coming from the kitchen in the morning, but today it seems strangely quiet.

Gradually, members of the household get up. Luster dresses Benjy. Dilsey starts a fire and prepares breakfast. Jason is upset. A window in his room has been broken, and he blames this on Luster and Benjy. Luster denies the charge.

Jason suddenly realizes that Miss Quentin has not gotten up. He wants her to be roused immediately. Dilsey protests that the young lady should be able to sleep late on Sunday, but Jason insists. Dilsey goes to call for Miss Quentin, but there is no answer. Jason comes and opens the door. The room turns out to be empty. The bed has not been slept in, and the window is open.

Dilsey says that Miss Quentin will return soon. Mrs Compson becomes convinced that Miss Quentin has committed suicide. She tells everyone to search for a note. Jason, however, rushes to his room, and retrieves a box from the closet.

He examines the box carefully, then goes to call the sheriff to report a robbery. At first, Jason threatens to report it to the governor if the sheriff does not follow his instructions. Since the law officer, apparently, is not intimidated, Jason says he will drive immediately to the sheriff's house. When Jason has left, Luster tells Dilsey that he and Benjy have seen Miss Quentin climb down the pear tree by her window every night.

Dilsey gets dressed for church, then she summons Luster. Benjy, who now lives mostly with the servants, goes with them to a negro church for the Easter service. Frony objects to his coming along, saying that people have begun to talk about it. Dilsey says that the only people to complain are "trash white folks." She adds that God does not care whether Benjy is bright or not.

Reverend Shegog, a famous minister from St. Louis, is scheduled to preach. He is small, aged and at first unimpressive. As the minister begins to speak, his manner is aloof and restrained. Soon, however, he takes the measure of his audience and his demeanor changes. He begins to speak in dialect, and he preaches a rousing sermon filled with apocalyptic imagery. The members of the congregation are profoundly moved.

After the sermon, Dilsey is in tears. Frony, concerned about what people will think, asks Dilsey to control herself. Her mother replies that she has seen the beginning and now sees the end. This refers, of course, to the Compson estate.

When Dilsey has changed and returned to the Compson household, Mrs Compson asks Dilsey if she has found the suicide

note from Miss Quentin. Mrs Compson is entirely convinced that Miss Quentin has killed herself. Dilsey repeats her conviction that Miss Quentin has just left temporarily. Mrs Compson, who has previously shown no interest in religion, asks Dilsey for a Bible.

The scene changes to the home of the sheriff, where Jason has just arrived. Jason has figured out that Miss Quentin and the travelling entertainer with a red tie have broken into his room and stolen thousands of dollars from him. He wants the sheriff to set out in immediate pursuit. Despite threats from Jason, the sheriff politely but firmly declines. He asks Jason for a detailed account of what happened, and says he will not get involved until there is proof that Miss Quentin and the entertainer performed the robbery. When Jason becomes belligerent, the sheriff says that Jason provoked Miss Quentin to run off. The sheriff asks why Jason kept thousands of dollars in his room, adding that he has suspicions about how Jason got the money.

Since no help is forthcoming, Jason starts off to pursue the couple by himself. After an exhausting journey, Jason finally comes to the town where the travelling company is currently performing. After finding what looks like the temporary camp of the performers, Jason spots the car in which the couple once drove by him. Jason asks an old man where Miss Quentin and the entertainer are. The man does not seem to know whom Jason is talking about, so Jason accuses the fellow of lying.

Jason grasps the man, who struggles to free himself and falls to the ground. The man is furious, and Jason no longer dares to let him go. Finally, Jason knocks the man down and runs toward his car. The old man follows him, swinging an axe. Jason grasps at the weapon. Suddenly, he feels a blow to the head. Half conscious, Jason finds himself in the company of members of the troop. He can still hear the furious voice of the old man in the distance.

The manager of the troop leads Jason around the corner, then tells him that he should leave. Jason, the manager says, had knocked his head against the rail, but the old man may kill him if he stays. Jason asks about his niece and the man with the red tie. The manager says that he has just fired them, since they were not the right sort of people for a respectable troop. Jason has no choice

but to leave. Too hurt to drive himself, he must hire somebody to
drive him home.

Later in the day, Jason is back at the Compson home. Luster
has been teasing Benjy by repeating "Caddy, Caddy," until Benjy
begins to cry. Dilsey reprimands her grandson. Luster gives Benjy
Caddy's slipper, which quiets him for a while. Then Benjy begins,
once more, to sob.

Dilsey wants to have Benjy taken for a ride in a carriage, but
T. P., who usually drives it, is not home. Luster volunteers to drive.
Once they are in the surrey, Benjy again grows calm. Luster mis-
chievously takes an unfamiliar route, causing Benjy to cry once
more. This disturbs Jason, who comes running up, strikes Luster
then directs the horse along the accustomed path. Benjy, once
more, grows quiet and serene.

Analysis

Since a part of the novel has been narrated from the viewpoint
of each of her siblings, we would expect the last part to be told by
Caddy. This is especially true because Caddy has been the focal
point of most of the action. The novel cannot be complete without
our knowing more about her point of view.

Caddy, as we have seen, plays so many different roles in the
novel that she is virtually impossible to characterize. To narrate a
part of the novel from her point of view would probably have been
impossible. Furthermore, even if it could be done, that would probably have destroyed the aura of mystery which surrounds Caddy
and is so important in the novel.

The sole daughter in the Compson family often embodies the
virtues of compassion and feminine wisdom. This is also true of
Dilsey, the figure around whom the section centers. Dilsey seems
to be standing in for Caddy. The section however, is not told from
the point of view of the aged cook but from that of an omniscient
narrator.

Faulkner probably could not have entered into the mind of
Dilsey very well. She is the only character in the book who is presented in a consistently positive way. In spite of this, much of her
interest for the reader, as with Caddy, lies in the way that she remains largely unknowable.

The last part is by far the most conventional section of the novel. Though less inspired than the previous three, it attempts to draw all of the highly divergent perspectives of the novel together into a coherent whole. The conclusion certainly does not succeed in this completely, but Faulkner, let us remember, called *The Sound and the Fury* his "most splendid failure."

The day is Easter Sunday, which is, according to Christian tradition, the time of Christ's resurrection. Symbols pertaining to Judgment Day and resurrection fill the entire novel. In the first part, for example, the entertainer in the red tie showed Benjy how he could put a lighted match in his mouth and close his lips. When he opened his lips again, the flame was still burning. The lighted match, we may realize in retrospect, was a symbol of the human soul, which dies and is resurrected.

Quentin constantly pondered death and resurrection. Flowers, symbols of Easter and resurrection, are frequently mentioned in the novel. This symbolism, however, is especially prevalent in the fourth section. It fills, for example, the apocalyptic sermon of Reverend Shegog.

But who, or what, is resurrected? To what does this symbolism refer? We know that the aristocratic Compson house is falling into ruin. Dilsey says that she now sees the end. But what do we see that promises rebirth?

For Jason, the events described in the novel are certainly a Day of Judgment. He must, quite literally, pay for his crimes, since his niece takes back the money stolen from her along with a little he has saved. He is left broke, with his reputation destroyed and even his job precarious.

Nevertheless, the end of the Compson house will mean that all the surviving people who have been stifled by the burden of its upkeep and traditions may be able to begin new lives. The best example, furthermore, may well be Jason himself, who faces death when the old man attacks him with an axe. For a moment, Jason's life seems to be over, but his rescue is like a resurrection. Because of this incident, he has a glimpse of where all of his rage may lead. For a while, at least, he appears more subdued. There is a possibility that his personality may change at last.

The rebirth can also refer to Miss Quentin, who takes the money and goes on to a new life. To an extent, this seems to be the resurrection that Mr, Quentin often pondered as he prepared for his suicide. Miss Quentin must have been born at just about the time of his death. She bears his name and must endure punishments for things he did. People, especially Benjy, often seem to equate the two. Mrs Compson identifies them so much that when Miss Quentin is missing she immediately starts to look for a suicide note.

Mr Quentin often imagined that he had committed incest with his sister Caddy. In all probability, that was just a fantasy, but it is symbolically important. Just as parents feel they continue in their children, Quentin seems to live on in his niece.

After all the drama of the book's events, a longing for order and stability remains. Luster, unlike Dilsey, has little or no understanding of what is taking place, but he can sense the tension that results. He takes it out on Benjy, uncharacteristically, by deliberately teasing him. When Dilsey orders Luster to take Benjy for a ride in the surrey, he takes an unfamiliar route, causing the retarded man to cry. Jason, ironically, comes to Benjy's rescue, restoring the familiar order by taking the reins of the horses. He threatens to kill Luster if the young man ever takes the wrong path again. The message is that, even now, familiar patterns cannot be changed too quickly.

Study Questions

1. What does Jason think at first when he finds that the window of his room has been broken?

2. What does Jason call Mrs Compson when she is slow about giving him the key to Miss Quentin's room?

3. What does Mrs Compson look for when she learns that Miss Quentin is missing?

4. What does Jason do as soon as he gets into Miss Quentin's room and finds the bed has not been slept in?

5. What does Luster tell Dilsey about Miss Quentin before they go to church?

6. What did Mrs Compson ask for after Dilsey returned from church?

7. Why did the sheriff refuse to help Jason pursue Miss Quentin and the travelling entertainer with a red tie?

8. Why was Jason so upset about the loss of his niece and of the money?

9. Where did Jason expect to find his niece and the man with the red tie?

10. What first starts Benjy crying in the afternoon?

Answers

1. When Jason finds the window in his room has been broken, he first thinks that Luster and Benjy are responsible.

2. When she is slow about giving him the key to Miss Quentin's room, Jason calls Mrs Compson an "old fool."

3. When she learns that Miss Quentin is missing, Mrs Compson looks for a suicide note.

4. When Jason gets into Miss Quentin's room and finds the bed has not been slept in, he runs to his room and checks the box where he keeps his money.

5. Before they go to church, Luster tells Dilsey that Miss Quentin climbs out of her room on a pear tree every night.

6. After Dilsey had returned from church, Mrs Compson asked for a Bible.

7. The sheriff refused to help Jason pursue Miss Quentin and the travelling entertainer with a red tie because there was no proof that they stole the money.

8. Jason was so upset about the loss of his niece and of the money because they symbolized compensation for the job and the opportunities which had been denied him.

9. Jason expected to find his niece and the man with the red tie in the car which he had followed the previous day.

10. Benjy first starts crying when a golfer uses the word "caddie," reminding him of his sister.

Suggested Essay Topics

1. There are parallels between the Compson family and the family of the negro servants. Frony, like Caddy, seems to have little contact with her child. Both young people, Luster and Miss Quentin, are being raised largely by their grandmothers. When she thinks Luster may have broken Jason's window, Dilsey says to her grandchild, "you got just es much Compson devilment in you es any of em." Do you think the family of servants shares any of the pathology of the Compsons? Make a detailed comparison of the two families, and state both the similarities and the differences.

2. It appears that Caddy has sometimes been seeing her daughter behind Jason's back, but we are told nothing about these meetings, or if, indeed, they took place at all. Miss Quentin insists on her right to the money Caddy left for her, but we know absolutely nothing about the relationship between mother and daughter. Do you think that Miss Quentin loves her mother or is the interest simply financial? When Miss Quentin tries to be more feminine, is this in imitation of her mother? What do you suppose they may have talked about? Why do you think this is not included in the novel? Compose a dialogue between Miss Quentin and Caddy.

3. The relationship between Mrs Compson and her brother, Uncle Maury, resembles the relationship between Jason and his sister, Caddy. In both cases, the brother uses his sister as a source of money. Does this indicate that Mrs Compson is correct when she says that Jason is really a Bascomb? Compare and contrast these two brother-sister relationships.

4. Flowers are a traditional symbol of Easter and resurrection, and they are mentioned often in the last part of *The Sound and the Fury*. When Jason meets Caddy at Mr Compson's funeral, she has placed flowers on the graves of her father and brother. There are flowers in the church where Rever-

end Shegog preaches. When Benjy begins crying, people give him a flower to calm him down. Look carefully at these and other references to flowers. Then discuss the various uses and meanings of flowers as a symbol.

5. At the end of the book, it seems very clear that the Compson house will have to change, but we do not know exactly how. What future do you see for Jason? For Dilsey? For Mrs Compson, Luster, Benjy and the others? What do you think will happen to Miss Quentin and the man with the red tie? What will Caddy do now that her financial burden has probably been eased?

Sample Analytical Paper Topics

Topic #1

The Significance of Names in Faulkner's *The Sound and the Fury*.

Outline

I. Thesis Statement: *Characters in* The Sound and the Fury *often attribute an enormous, even magical, power to names. Dilsey, for example, in the first part, says her name is written in heaven and will be called on the Judgment Day. Very often, the name is regarded as a part of the person, no more separable than the heart or brain. This, however, is not unusual. Artists or leaders seek immortality through a name that will be repeated after death. By such acts as banning the name of Caddy or changing the original name of Benjy, Mrs Compson, especially, seems to be trying to conjure with names. Compare the various ways that names are used by characters in Faulkner's* The Sound and the Fury.

II. The importance of names

    A. A name as a means to immortality

    B. The name as a part of the human being

III. The changing of Benjy's original name

    A. Why Mrs Compson did not want Benjy to be named after her brother

    B. Why Mrs Compson selected the new name of "Benjamin"

        1. Benjamin in the Old Testament

        2. The Old Testament family of Benjamin compared to the Compsons

    C. Reactions to the name change

        1. The reaction of Caddy

        2. The reaction of Dilsey

        3. The reaction of Roskus

        4. The reaction of Versh

    D. How people called the son "Benjy" instead of "Benjamin"

        1. How "Benjy" sounded like "Maury"

        2. How Mrs Compson considered nicknames vulgar

        3. Why everyone persisted in using "Benjy"

IV. How Caddy's name was banished from the Compson house

    A. How Mrs Compson insisted the name never be used

        1. How Mrs Compson did not want Miss Quentin to know about her mother

        2. How Mrs Compson felt Caddy had taken over as mother

    B. How the ban on Caddy's name did not work

        1. How Benjy thought of his sister whenever a golfer said "caddie"

        2. How everyone thought about and remembered Caddy even without saying her name

V. How the name of Quentin lived on

    A. Why Miss Quentin was named after her Uncle

        1. Caddy was very close to Quentin

        2. Caddy may have wanted to guarantee that Quentin's name not be banned from the Compson household

    B. How Mr Quentin's name lived on in Miss Quentin

1. How Miss Quentin was born only a few months after Mr Quentin died

2. How Miss Quentin was punished for what Quentin had done

3. How Benjy sometimes seemed to equate Mr Quentin with Miss Quentin

4. How Mrs Compson assumed that Miss Quentin had committed suicide, like her son

VI. Conclusions: Names are significant in this book

   A. How names influence the way people are treated

   B. The importance of being able to look beyond names

Topic #2

The Significance of time in Faulkner's *The Sound and the Fury.*

Outline

I. Thesis Statement: *People have disagreed over the nature of time. One philosopher of ancient Greece, Heraclitus, maintained that change was the ultimate reality, while another, Parmenides, believed that time was an illusion. The debate was very intense when Faulkner wrote, just as it is today. Faulkner was influenced by the French philosopher Heri Bergson, who emphasized the transient nature of all things, but he was also attracted to a Christian view of time as only a gateway to eternity.*

In The Sound and the Fury *Faulkner uses various characters to represent different views of the nature of time. Compare and contrast these various perspectives. Which do you think Faulkner considered closest to the truth? Which, if any, do you believe is right?*

II. What is time?

   A. Is permanence an illusion?

   B. Is change an illusion?

III. Time in the perspective of Benjy

      A.   How there is no time—no past, present or future—for Benjy

      B.   Benjy is upset by any threat of change

IV.   Time in the perspective of Mr Compson

      A.   How change is the only reality for Mr Compson

      B.   How Mr Compson looks to time for relief of his misery

      C.   How Mr Compson feels threatened by permanence

      D.   The nihilism of Mr Compson

V.   Time in the perspective of Quentin

      A.   How Quentin tries to escape time

      B.   How Quentin tries to understand time

      C.   How Quentin breaks his watch to overcome time

      D.   How Quentin commits suicide to overcome time

VI.   Time in the perspective of Jason

      A.   How Jason lives completely in time

      B.   How Jason is haunted by the past

      C.   How Jason reacts in the present

      D.   How Jason has no vision of the future

VII. Time in the perspective of Dilsey

      A.   The devout Christianity of Dilsey and its effect on her perception of time

      B.   How Dilsey lives in the present

      C.   How Dilsey is not troubled by the past

      D.   How Dilsey regards time as a passage to eternity

VIII. Time in the perspective of other major characters

      A.   How Mrs Compson wants to preserve the past

      B.   How Caddy wants to escape the past

IX.   Conclusions: The nature of time

    A.   Which view of time, if any, did Faulkner accept

    B.   Which view of time, if any, should we accept

Topic #3

Family Relationships in Faulkner's *The Sound and the Fury*.

Outline

I.   Thesis Statement: *Faulkner always insisted on the vital importance of family, yet the family relationships in his work tend to be very turbulent.* The Sound and the Fury *provides many excellent examples of this. Explore the important family relationships in the novel systematically. Some we learn nothing about, but others are described in various degrees of detail. Analyze why most of them are so troubled and how they might have been improved.*

II.   Families in *The Sound and the Fury*

    A.   The Compson Family

    B.   The Gibson Family

    C.   The Bascomb Family

III.   Husband-wife relationships in *The Sound and the Fury*

    A.   Jason II and Caroline Compson

    B.   Dilsey and Roskus Gibson

    C.   Caddy and Herbert Head

IV.   Mother-son relationships in *The Sound and the Fury*

    A.   Mrs Compson and Quentin

    B.   Mrs Compson and Benjy

    C.   Mrs Compson and Jason

    D.   Mrs Bland and Gerald Bland

    E.   Frony and Luster

V.   Mother-daughter relationships in *The Sound and the Fury*

    A.   Mrs Compson and Caddy

    B.   Caddy and Miss Quentin

    C.   Dilsey and Frony

VI.   Father-son relationships in *The Sound and the Fury*

    A.   Mr Compson and Quentin

    B.   Mr Compson and Benjy

    C.   Mr Compson and Jason

VII. Brother-sister relationships in *The Sound and the Fury*

    A.   Caddy and Benjy

    B.   Caddy and Quentin

    C.   Caddy and Jason

    D.   Mrs Compson and Uncle Maury

VIII. Brother-brother relationships in *The Sound and the Fury*

    A.   Benjy and Quentin

    B.   Benjy and Jason

    C.   Quentin and Jason

IX.   Grandparent-grandchild relationships in *The Sound and the Fury*

    A.   Damuddy and Jason

    B.   Damuddy and Quentin

    C.   Damuddy and Benjy

    D.   Damuddy and Caddy

    E.   Mrs Compson and Miss Quentin

    F.   Dilsey and Luster

X.   Sister-sister relationships in *The Sound and the Fury*

    A.   There are no sister-sister relationships in *The Sound and the Fury*

    B.   Did Faulkner have special difficulty imagining or representing such relationships?

XI. What can we learn about families from *The Sound and the Fury*

    A. Which family relationships prove most troubled?

    B. Which family relationships prove least troubled?

    C. How might the families have been improved?

Appendix:

Chronology of Major Events in *The Sound and the Fury*

circa 1889—The birth of Quentin Compson.

circa 1891—The birth of Candace (Caddy) Compson.

circa 1893—The birth of Jason IV Compson.

April 7, 1895—The birth of Benjamin Compson (formerly "Maury," called "Benjy").

Fall 1898—The death of Damuddy.

circa 1900—Benjamin Compson's name changed from "Maury Compson."

April 25, 1910—The marriage of Candace Compson to Herbert Head.

May 1910—The castration of Benjamin Compson after he runs after some young girls.

June 2, 1910—The date of the narration in Part Two of the novel; the suicide of Quentin Compson.

circa Fall 1910—Herbert Head discovers the pregnancy of Candace and abandons her.

circa Winter 1910—The birth of Miss Quentin, daughter of Candace Compson; Miss Quentin is brought home to the Compson estate by Mr (Jason III) Compson.

circa 1912—The death of Mr (Jason III) Compson, brought on by alcoholism; Jason IV and Candace Compson meet at the grave of Jason III, and Candace begins sending money for the care of Miss Quentin.

circa 1914—The death of Roskus Gibson.

April 6, 1918—Date of the narration in Part Three of the novel.

April 7, 1928—Date of the narration in Part One of the novel.

April 8, 1928—Date of the narration in Part Four of the novel; Miss Quentin takes the money that Jason kept in a box and runs away with a travelling entertainer.

SECTION EIGHT

Bibliography

Adams, Richard P. *Faulkner: Myth and Motion.* Princeton: Princeton University Press, 1968.

Bloom, Harold, ed. *William Faulkner's The Sound and the Fury.* New York: Chelsea House, 1988.

Brodhead, Richard H., ed. *Faulkner: New Perspectives.* Englewood Cliffs, NJ: Prentice Hall, 1983.

Brooks, Cleanth. *William Faulkner: First Encounters.* New Haven: Yale University Press, 1983.

Faulkner, William. *The Sound and the Fury.* New York: Vintage, 1984.

Crunden, Robert M. *A Brief History of American Culture.* New York: Paragon House, 1994.

Polk, Noel, ed. *New Essays on The Sound and the Fury.* New York: Cambridge University Press, 1993.

Warren, Robert Penn, ed. *Faulkner: A Collection of Critical Essays.* Englewood Cliffs, NJ: Prentice Hall, 1966.